NUOVO
MONDO

New Italian Food

This book is dedicated to all of those who have made Stefano's a great restaurant over the past 20 years. Special thanks to Rosalie Langdon and Peter Webley.

Published in 2012 by Hardie Grant Books

Hardie Grant Books (Australia)
Ground Floor, Building 1
658 Church Street
Richmond, Victoria 3121
www.hardiegrant.com.au

Hardie Grant Books (UK)
Dudley House, North Suite
34–35 Southampton Street
London WC2E 7HF
www.hardiegrant.co.uk

A Cataloguing-in-Publication entry is available from the catalogue of the National Library of Australia at www.nla.gov.au

Nuovo Mondo
ISBN 9781742703824

Publishing Director: Paul McNally
Project Editor: Hannah Koelmeyer
Editors: Foong Ling Kong and Jacqueline Blanchard
Design Manager: Heather Menzies
Designers: Gayna Murphy and Vivien Valk
Photographer: Alan Benson
Stylist: Deborah Kaloper
Production: Penny Sanderson

Colour reproduction by Splitting Image Colour Studio
Printed and bound in China by 1010 Printing International Limited

NUOVO MONDO

New Italian Food

Stefano de Pieri
Jim McDougall

hardie grant books
MELBOURNE · LONDON

contents

introduction

Stefano ‿ Like all cuisines, Italian cooking is bound to be interpreted and reinterpreted by many cooks, depending on where they live or where their imagination takes them. Italian cooks in Australia have remained, by and large, faithful to tradition. Some have excelled within that context while some continue to offer dishes that compromise Italian flavours in response to commercial needs.

My cooking has remained pretty firmly in the conservative camp, sticking to tradition and an idea of purity and simplicity. There will always be a place for *spaghetti al burro* and *parmigiano*, lamb *al forno* and for the marvellous *crostatas* served with homemade jam, all of which have stood the test of time.

But times they are a-changin', like Dylan said, and it is impossible to remain immune to new methods, innovations or flights of culinary fancy. Australian contemporary chefs have embraced almost everything culinary; experimenting widely with cooking styles and techniques to produce some amazing results, gaining new insights into the possibilities of restaurant food and, above all, identifying new and exciting flavours.

Jim turned my comfortable world upside-down ater returning to Mildura after a five-year stint working with Shannon Bennet in Melbourne. I have published three books and been at the stove without significant interruption for some twenty years. Not many cooks stay in the same place like I have – looking after my customers has always been my focus and my motto.

With that, however, comes a certain amount of repetition and a tendency to stay safe. The arrival of the young buck Jim has shaken me from some complacency, as this book will endeavour to show.

Nuovo Mondo may appear somewhat different to my previous books which illustrate standard Italian fare. If, however, you are looking for something a little new, this book is for you.

These ideas are not difficult to implement. On the odd occasion we have mentioned truffles and crayfish (expensive, but easily found), but by and large, we have stayed well within the realm of what is possible for the home cook. The food may not 'look' Italian – but what does Italian look like now? Have you seen the food prepared by contemporary Italian chefs in Italy?

Jim and I hope *Nuovo Mondo* will help, in a modest way, to inspire a new generation of Italian chefs.

Jim ⁓ I believe great food is born out of great ideas. It doesn't matter what the cuisine or which country it hails from, my philosophy is that good food comes from within an individual and the presence of soul in a dish is often more important than technique.

There is no better example of that, for me, than Italian cuisine. A cuisine where there is no hero complex, no reason to show off and a complete adherence to tradition and an unparalleled respect for produce.

This book shows both sides of the cooking spectrum, the simple and the complicated. I love nothing more than to create a dish that is flamboyant and complex; the need to satisfy every sense and explore every texture is an essential quality of a fine-dining chef. But I am aware that the focus is constantly shifting; for instance, today, molecular gastronomy is starting to fade and chefs are rediscovering the true sense of food and the importance of simplicity.

Cuisine today is becoming lighter, purer and a lot more healthy. I can think of nothing worse than eating out and being so full that I can hardly move. In saying that, it is equally bad leaving a restaurant after paying a fortune and still feeling hungry. It is all about balance.

Food is becoming more ingredient-driven than technique-driven. The emphasis is on not overshadowing a great product with unnecessary complications. This flexible environment enables chefs to borrow from other cuisines in order to create a menu. It is not unusual to see miso or yuzu in a French restaurant or to garnish an Italian dish with a bit of coriander. In my mind this is the essence of modern Australian cuisine.

Nuovo Mondo aims to explore just that. I am Australian and have had the pleasure of working with some great Italian chefs, but I have also had the opportunity to work with incredible chefs from many different cultures. I still hold Italian food values in the highest regard and although I may have different ideals at times, I keep coming back to the beauty of simplicity that makes Italian cuisine great.

The marriage between the two styles in this book is plainly evident. There is a clear trail from Stefano's world into mine, and in our selection of recipes we've attempted to balance enthusiasm and maturity. To me, fun and passion are prerequisites to a fulfilling life. The ideas explored in this book are designed to enhance your creativity as a cook and also to showcase a broad range of dishes – don't take it too seriously – just laugh and cook.

antipasto &
first course

Jim~

Good antipasto is one of the most important elements of an Italian meal, where adaptable and simple ideas are designed to engage and entice the diner. The first course, in my opinion, should be light, small and full of flavour.

Antipasto is perfect for exploring flavours that you may not be able to incorporate into a main course. Complementary components are key here. You must always treat your main ingredient with love – it has to taste amazing – then the elements that you add to it will make the distinction between a mediocre dish and one that will be special and memorable.

Stefano~

I like to think of antipasto as being like a big space where you are allowed to play any game you like. Jim has introduced some ideas here that go beyond the usual offerings of prosciutto, olives, sun-dried tomatoes and salumi. There's nothing wrong with these ingredients, as long as they are the result of a genuine effort, either in the kitchen or, even more importantly, in the sourcing and manufacturing of the food.

Nothing is more depressing to me than antipasto items produced for the mass market. It is better by far to make your own simple frittata than buy ready-made dishes that use poor-quality ingredients.

I have chased Jim around this section with some more traditional and classic antipasto ideas to complement some of his more ebullient and flamboyant recipes.

Fried Bread with Parmesan Mousse

This makes delicious finger food, but could also be eaten as a starter, in which case we'd argue for a small salad to be added to the table. Here we suggest using red-and-white witlof (chicory) as well as curly endive, pomegranate seeds and a dressing of Greek-style yoghurt diluted with a little olive oil. The acidity of the yoghurt and pomegranate should be enough to carry the flavour – if it's not sharp enough, add a little lemon juice. Leftover mousse is good for melting over potatoes or as a dip with crusty bread or biscuits.

Makes 20 pieces, serves 4–6

8 cups (2 litres/70 fl oz) vegetable oil
1 quantity Simple Pizza Dough (page 194)

Parmesan Mousse

1½ cups (150 g/5½ oz) grated Parmigiano
    Reggiano cheese
1 cup (250 ml/9 fl oz) Béchamel Sauce
    (page 187)
50 ml (1¾ fl oz) pouring (whipping) cream
¼ bunch chives, snipped
1 clove garlic, finely crushed
salt and freshly ground black pepper

To make the Parmesan Mousse, add the cheese to the Béchamel Sauce while it is hot in the pan, and whisk to combine. Set aside to cool completely. Whip the cream to soft peaks, then fold into the béchamel, along with the chives and garlic, using a rubber spatula. Season with salt and pepper. Spoon the mixture into a piping bag fitted with a 5 mm (¼ inch) nozzle and set aside until required.

Preheat the oil to 180°C (350°F) in a deep-fryer or large heavy-based saucepan. Test the oil by dropping a little dough in it – if it sizzles furiously it is hot enough.

Divide the pizza dough into 4 equal pieces. If you own a pasta machine, turn the setting to 3 and roll out the dough in sheets – each should be about 5 mm (¼ inch) thick. If you don't own a pasta machine, use a rolling pin to roll the dough into a rectangle.

Cut the dough into 5 cm (2 inch) squares. Gently lower each square of dough, one by one, into the hot oil – the dough should puff up and start to get crisp. Flip the pieces every now and then as they cook to ensure even cooking. When crisp, remove from the oil and drain on paper towel.

Using a small knife, make a small hole in one side of each piece of fried bread, just large enough to fit the piping nozzle. Fill each bread puff with mousse, and serve.

Stefano ⁓ *If you prefer to avoid frying the bread, these puffs can be baked in a 200°C (390°F) oven for 3–4 minutes.*

Artichoke Crisps with Anchovy Salt

This is an impressive little snack to pull out when friends drop by.
It is a healthier alternative to fried potato chips, especially if you use unsaturated oil.
You can use almost any root vegetable as a substitute. The crisps keep well
in an airtight container for up to a week.

To make the Anchovy Salt, preheat the oven to 130°C (250°F/Gas 1).
Place the anchovies on a tray lined with baking paper and bake for
4 hours, or until the anchovies are completely dry (a dehydrator is
great for this if you have one). Place the dried anchovies in a mortar
and pound with the pestle until they become an oily powder. Add
the salt and stir gently to combine, but try not to break up the
flakes of salt.

Preheat the oil to 160°C (315°F) in a deep-fryer or large heavy-
based saucepan. Test the oil by dropping a little bread in it – if it
sizzles furiously it is hot enough.

Remove the tough outer leaves of the artichokes. No other trimming is
required as the artichoke will be so thinly sliced that the actual choke,
which is usually discarded, will not be a problem. Cut the artichokes
lengthwise on a mandoline or use a meat slicer to slice them as thinly
as possible, about 3 mm (⅛ inch) thick. (This is very difficult to do by
hand, so if you don't have a mandoline or meat slicer, use a softer root
vegetable, such as sweet potato or Jerusalem artichoke.)

Lightly toss the sliced artichoke in the rice flour to coat. Deep-fry
the artichoke chips, in batches, until crisp but not too dark. Drain
on paper towel. Season with the anchovy salt and serve as a pre-
dinner snack.

Serves 4–6

vegetable oil, for deep-frying
3 globe artichokes
1¼ cups (220 g/7¾ oz) rice flour

Anchovy Salt
1 x 45 g (1¾ oz) tin good-quality anchovy
    fillets
¾ cup (100 g/3½ oz) salt flakes

Pancetta with Smoked Provolone, Grilled Polenta and Quail Eggs

Jim ⁓ This dish came about during a conversation between me and Stefano that started with a series of 'What ifs' and ended with this dish. We were doing a function at a high-end Italian provedore in Melbourne and decided the pancetta was too good to be grilled or cooked. We decided it should only be used as a 'table pancetta' and Stefano said 'How good would it be with a bit of grilled polenta and some of that smoked provolone?' Not to be outdone, I suggested quail eggs also be added. And so a dish was born.

Preheat the griller (broiler) to high.

Place the polenta on a baking tray, with the cheese on top.

Place the tray under the hot griller until the cheese melts. Arrange a polenta piece on each serving plate, then immediately place 3 slices of pancetta on top of each portion so the pancetta wilts a bit from the heat of the polenta.

Cut each quail egg in half – the yolks should be beautiful and runny but still holding their shape – and arrange on top of the polenta and pancetta. Drizzle with a little extra-virgin olive oil and season with salt and pepper.

Serves 4

Polenta (page 195), cut into 10 cm × 4 cm
(4 inch × 1½ inch) rectangles
4 slices smoked provolone or similar
smoked cheese, cut into
13 cm × 7 cm (5 inch × 2¾ inch) strips
12 paper-thin slices pancetta
6 Boiled Quail Eggs (page 187)
extra-virgin olive oil, for drizzling
salt and freshly ground black pepper

Stefano ⁓ I could eat polenta for breakfast! On a recent trip to Italy during mushroom season I was reminded how good polenta and funghi are together. I suggest, instead of the egg in this dish, cooking an array of mushrooms in a little butter, olive oil and garlic. Unruly mushrooms all over the pretty pieces of polenta with hand-torn fresh parsley and a crank of black pepper may look a bit messier but will taste just as marvellous. You can also replace the smoked provolone with an unsmoked cheese, and you can omit the pancetta to end up with a fabulous vegetarian dish.

Bruschetta of Smashed Broad Beans with Pecorino and Lemon

We wait with anticipation for the first broad beans of the season, when they are young and tender – at this stage you do not need to remove the outer skin of each bean as you may have to when they are a bit older. The utter simplicity of this antipasto is what makes it so attractive.

Serves 4–6

1 cup (185 g/6½ oz) small podded broad (fava) beans
½ cup (40 g/1½ oz) finely diced pecorino cheese
extra-virgin olive oil, for drizzling
salt
juice of ½ lemon
8–12 slices ciabatta

Place the broad beans and pecorino in a large mortar and use a pestle to pound them together, drizzling in the olive oil until you have a coarse paste. Adjust with salt and a touch of lemon juice, to taste.

Toast the ciabatta under a hot griller (broiler), or preferably over a fire if you can be bothered (this gives the bread a pleasantly smoky flavour), until crisp.

Spread about 1 tablespoon of the broad bean mixture over each slice of toasted bread. Garnish with a drizzle of olive oil to serve.

Smoked Wagyu with Horseradish Mayonnaise and Pickled Radish

Full-blood wagyu is perfect for this dish; the marbling gives a depth of flavour that is hard to beat. In the restaurant, we use Blackmore wagyu from Alexandria in Victoria's high country. The Blackmores' passion for their product is unparalleled and the meat never disappoints. A good-quality grain-fed beef is a great substitute. The meat takes a few days to cure, so start at least three days in advance. You can use a smaller cut of meat, but it will not be as good; my advice is to make more than you'll need and keep it for another use.

Put the smoking chips in a deep roasting tray. Place the beef in a perforated baking tray that will fit inside the roasting tray with the chips. Stack the trays, cover with foil and place over high heat until the chips are smoking furiously. You can use a stovetop but this may smoke out your house, so an outdoor barbecue is the best option. Turn off the heat and leave for 20 minutes for the smoke to infuse. Turn the beef over and repeat this smoking step three or four times until the beef smells very smoky.

Coat the beef with the pepper and rosemary. Combine the sugar and salt in a large plastic container, then bury the beef in the mixture. Cover and place in the refrigerator to cure for 2 days.

Rinse the beef under cold water. Place on a tray and leave it unwrapped in the refrigerator for a further 2 days. It can be eaten immediately, but the air-drying improves the texture of the beef.

To make the Pickled Radish, place the radishes in a deep bowl. Put the remaining ingredients into a saucepan and bring to the boil, then pour the hot liquid over the radishes and set aside to pickle for 2 hours.

To serve, very thinly slice the meat and arrange on a platter. Top with the Horseradish Mayonnaise and pickled radish, and garnish with wild mustard leaves and a sprinkling of capers. Drizzle with loads of good olive oil.

Serves 25

100 g (3½ oz) wood smoking chips
2–3 kg (4 lb 8 oz–6 lb 12 oz) piece wagyu girello, trimmed of sinew
100 g (3½ oz) freshly ground black pepper
2 sprigs rosemary, roughly chopped
2¾ cups (630 g/1 lb 5 oz) caster (superfine) sugar
1.4 kg (3 lb 2 oz) salt
Horseradish Mayonnaise (see Variation, page 188), to serve
wild mustard leaves, to garnish
2 tablespoons lilliput capers, rinsed and drained, to garnish
extra-virgin olive oil, for drizzling

Pickled Radish
1 bunch radishes, stems trimmed to 1 cm (½ inch)
1⅓ cups (310 g/11 oz) caster (superfine) sugar
600 ml (21 fl oz) white vinegar
1 bay leaf
4 whole black peppercorns

Battered Oysters with Fennel and Pear Salad

Jim ~ A nicely battered oyster can be quite special. Coupled with a lovely salad, it is fun to eat and exciting to taste. When I was suddenly plunged into a job as head chef, I was constantly trying to find exciting dishes that were both great in flavour and cost effective. This dish ticks both boxes. Because the oyster is cooked it doesn't have to be freshly shucked. This recipe is designed as an antipasto, two oysters per portion. For a starter, allow half a dozen oysters per diner.

Combine the salt and 3 tablespoons water in a bowl to make 'wet salt'.

Remove the oysters from their shells. Refrigerate the oysters until needed, and rinse and reserve the shells for serving.

To make the Red Wine Vinaigrette, combine the vinegar, olive oil and sugar in a small saucepan over medium heat and stir until the sugar dissolves. Allow to cool, then stir in the chives and set aside.

To make a batter, combine the flours in a medium-sized bowl, reserving a little plain flour for dusting the oysters. Add the iced water and a pinch of salt, and mix very gently. The batter should be lumpy – pockets of flour are great for this batter.

Preheat the oil to 180°C (350°F) in a deep-fryer or large heavy-based saucepan. Test the oil by dropping a little batter in it – if it sizzles furiously it is hot enough.

Dust the oyster meat first in the reserved plain flour, then dip into the batter. Deep-fry the oysters, in batches, until crisp and light golden.

To serve, place 12 mounds of the wet salt on a serving plate and arrange an oyster shell over each mound.

Divide the fennel and pear between the shells, drizzle each with about 1 tablespoon of vinaigrette. Place an oyster on top and serve.

Serves 6

100 g (3½ oz) salt
12 oysters, on the half shell
100 g (3½ oz) rice flour
⅔ cup (100 g/3½ oz) plain (all-purpose) flour
2 cups (500 ml/17 fl oz) iced water
vegetable oil, for deep-frying
1 head baby fennel, julienned
1 nashi pear, peeled, cored and cut into
    matchstick batons

Red Wine Vinaigrette
50 ml (1¾ fl oz) red wine vinegar
2 tablespoons extra-virgin olive oil
2 tablespoons caster (superfine) sugar
½ bunch chives, snipped

Stefano ~ I am so fond of oysters I dream of eating several dozen in one sitting; only decorum prevents me from doing so! Freshly shucked oysters are good with eggs. Scramble eggs in a little butter until barely set and spoon a dollop over as many oysters as you like. A few salmon eggs or – bliss if you can afford it – a little caviar on top will finish it off perfectly. I like a dry prosecco to drink with this as it is mellow and the bubbles are not too intrusive. What is appealing about this little dish is the extraordinary contrast between the briny, salty, cold oyster and the hot, soft, gooey eggs topped with the fish eggs that burst in the mouth.

Potato Terrine with Anchovy and Rosemary

This is a great summer dish . If you omit the anchovies, this terrine makes a perfect vegetarian starter, especially if served with a crisp green salad.

Serves 10–20

4 cups (1 litre/35 fl oz) full-cream
    (whole) milk
3 bay leaves
1 small handful thyme
3 teaspoons salt
6 cloves garlic
8 small waxy potatoes, such as Sebago,
    peeled and cut into 3 mm (⅛ inch) slices
150 ml (5 fl oz) Clarified Butter
    (page 186)
10 good-quality anchovy fillets, cut in
    half lengthwise, plus extra for garnish
salt flakes

Rosemary Dressing
1 tablespoon capers, rinsed and drained
2 bunches rosemary
⅓ cup (80 ml/2½ fl oz) olive oil
2 tablespoons balsamic vinegar

To make the terrine, put the milk, bay leaves, thyme, salt and garlic in a large saucepan over medium heat. As soon as the milk comes to the boil, add the potato slices and cook until tender but not mushy (you may need to do this in batches) – they should still be a bit firm. Remove the potatoes and set aside once cooked.

Line a 20 cm × 10 cm (8 inch × 4 inch) terrine tin or mould with baking paper. While the potatoes are still warm, start layering them into the tin. After each layer is complete, brush a thin layer of Clarified Butter on the potatoes and scatter with a few anchovy halves. Repeat until all of the potato is used, then cover with plastic wrap and place a similar-sized tin on top with a weight inside (food tins work well for this) to weight it down. Refrigerate for about 2 hours, or until set.

To make the Rosemary Dressing, put the capers and rosemary in a mortar and use a pestle to pound them until coarse and fragrant. Mix in the oil and vinegar and set aside until required.

To serve, remove the terrine from the refrigerator, uncover and turn out onto a chopping board. Cut into 10 cm × 3 cm (4 inch × 1¼ inch) pieces. Season with salt flakes, garnish with the remaining anchovy halves and spoon some rosemary dressing over the top.

Stefano ⁓ *A little salad of perfect, crunchy green leaves goes beautifully with this terrine. You could also add a garnish of tuna – simply cut a 2 cm (¾ inch) cube of tuna (80 g per person is ample). Heat a little extra-virgin olive oil in a non-stick pan, then add a sprig of rosemary and a crushed garlic clove. sizzle for 1 minute or less, then sear the tuna quickly to colour it on each side, season and serve, discarding the garlic and rosemary.*

Stefano's Artichoke Salad

My daughter, Claudia, never used to like parmesan cheese. When she returned after a long stay in Italy, she brought with her with a recipe for a salad with artichokes and Parmigiano Reggiano (not Grana, its cousin) to which she had become addicted. This salad requires the best firm, fresh artichokes. These are served free of the choke; the hairy inside which makes them unpalatable.

Snap off the tough outer leaves of the artichokes until your reach the paler tender ones, then use a small sharp knife to peel around the base and trim the stem. Cut away the top one-third of the globe then slice them finely, avoiding the hairy choke. Spread the slices over a flat plate.

Scatter the lemon juice over the artichoke to stop it from discolouring, then sprinkle over the salt flakes and Parmigiano Reggiano. Drizzle with extra-virgin olive oil to taste, and add more lemon juice, if desired. Serve at once as part of an antipasto.

Serves 2–3

4 young globe artichokes
juice of 2 small lemons
salt flakes
1 cup (100 g/3½ oz) shaved Parmigiano
   Reggiano cheese
extra-virgin olive oil, for drizzling

Stefano ‿ This is one of those dishes where the pitfalls are many. To be successful, every element of the dish must be perfect. Simple dishes like this one require the best ingredients and that takes effort. Use good-quality extra-virgin olive oil and try to find artichokes in season – avoid any that are old, dried up and filled with 'chokes'. Not all lemons are the same – you will notice how they change in Australia during the summer month, because when out of season they are imported from other parts of the world and the flavour is inferior. Salt flakes are essential for the best flavour – ordinary table salt is too salty for this dish!

Duck Egg Frittata with Salted Onion, Old Balsamic and Green Olives

Jim ⁓ I always say it is much easier to mess up the simple dishes than the complicated ones, because with simple dishes there is nowhere to hide your mistakes. In this dish, Stefano's technique of emulsifying olive oil into the eggs is what makes this frittata exceptional. This version is based on one of his old recipes, but instead of baking extra ingredients into the frittata, I have used them as a garnish. If duck eggs are not available you can substitute fifteen free-range hen's eggs.

Serves 6

8–10 duck eggs
¼ cup (60 ml/2 fl oz) extra-virgin olive oil, plus extra to serve
¼ cup (60 ml/2 fl oz) pouring (whipping) cream
½ cup (50 g/1¾ oz) grated Parmigiano Reggiano cheese
1 teaspoon freshly grated nutmeg
1 clove garlic, crushed
salt and freshly ground black pepper
12 pitted green olives, sliced, to serve
good-quality aged balsamic vinegar, for drizzling

Parsley Chips
½ tablespoon olive oil
1 handful of flat-leaf (Italian) parsley
a pinch of salt

Salted Onion
2 large onions, very thinly sliced
1½ tablespoons salt
2 tablespoons good-quality aged balsamic vinegar

Preheat the oven to 100°C (200°F/Gas ½). Line a 15 cm × 30 cm (6 inch × 12 inch) baking dish with baking paper.

To make the frittata, whisk the eggs, then incorporate the olive oil and beat well to emulsify. Mix in the cream, parmesan, nutmeg and garlic until combined. Pour into the prepared dish and bake for 2–3 hours, or until the frittata is set – the low temperature will create a bubble-free frittata. Remove from the oven and allow to cool in the tray for at least 30 minutes before turning out.

Meanwhile, make the Parsley Chips. Tightly cover an old dinner plate with plastic wrap. Lightly oil the plastic wrap and place the parsley leaves on top, ensuring they sit flat. Scatter with a little salt and microwave on high for 3 minutes. Remove and check the parsley; it should be crisp. If not, return to the microwave and cook for a further 2 minutes. (The parsley can be fried in a small pot of oil, but your chips will be darker.) Drain on paper towel and set aside; do not refrigerate.

To make the Salted Onion, combine the onion and salt in a large bowl and set aside to marinate for at least 30 minutes. Rinse the onion under cold running water, then drain well. Stir through the balsamic vinegar and set aside.

To serve, cut the frittata into slices and arrange on serving plates. Place the onion on top and garnish with the parsley chips and olives. Drizzle with balsamic vinegar and extra-virgin olive oil.

Mozzarella

Jim ⁓ My friend Davide Barbisan, used to make Mozzarella in Carrozza on the paddle steamer *Avoca* when we both lived in Mildura and I was a young, impressionable cook. His food inspired me, not because it was technically amazing but because it was so perfect in its simplicity and freshness, and always presented itself as a benchmark to my own cooking. My Mozzarella in Pizza Dough (page 26) is a homage to Davide's recipe. I have adapted it using pizza dough, and although the recipe is a departure from the original, it is great to eat and good fun to make.

Stefano ～ These Mozzarella in Carrozza (page 27) are made using a 'live' culture batter that needs to be treated as if it were a child; feed in the morning and the evening. My recipe is for a quick batter with only one feed, but for the best results, make the batter two days (four feeds) before you use it. The batter can be used for anything you wish to deep-fry. The recipe was given to us by a chef who worked at Stefano's, Davide Barbisan, and it has been kept and used by another Stefano's stalwart, Ashley Allford, who kindly supplied it to us again.

Jim's Mozzarella in Pizza Dough with Anchovy and Caper Dressing

Serves 4

8 good-quality anchovy fillets
16 baby bocconcini
1 quantity Simple Pizza Dough
    (page 194)
2 free-range egg yolks, lightly
    whisked
sesame seeds, for sprinkling

Anchovy and Caper Dressing
100 g (3½ oz) butter, melted
3 good-quality anchovy fillets,
    finely chopped
1 tablespoon capers, rinsed and
    drained
2 tablespoon red wine vinegar

Preheat the oven to 190°C (375°F/Gas 5). Line a baking tray with baking paper.

Cut the anchovies in half crosswise and, using your thumb, push one into the centre of each bocconcini.

Divide the pizza dough into 16 equal-sized portions and roll out into rounds. Place a bocconcini in the middle of each round. Bring the dough up over each bocconcini, fold over at the top, then press together to seal and enclose the bocconcini.

Place the bocconcini balls, seam side down, on the prepared tray. Lightly brush the egg yolk over the top of each to coat, then sprinkle with sesame seeds. Leave to prove in a warm place for 5 minutes.

Bake the cheese balls in the oven for 10–15 minutes, or until golden and crisp.

Meanwhile, make the Anchovy and Caper Dressing. Heat a small saucepan over high heat and, when it is very hot, add the butter and cook until brown and nutty. Add the anchovy and capers – they will sizzle a little bit when you add them. Remove from the heat and set aside to cool, then add the vinegar and stir to combine.

Serve the warm mozzarella balls drizzled with the anchovy and caper dressing.

Stefano's Mozzarella in Carrozza

Makes 6

6 thick slices fresh mozzarella
  cheese
12 good-quality anchovy fillets
3 slices white bread, crusts removed
  and cut into 5 cm (2 inch)
  squares
300 ml (10½ fl oz) full-cream (whole)
  milk
vegetable oil, for deep-frying

Batter
3¾ cups (560 g/1 lb 4 oz) plain
  (all-purpose) flour
205 g (7¼ oz) white sugar
3 teaspoons salt flakes
1½ teaspoons dry yeast

To make the batter, combine 3 cups (450 g/1 lb) of the flour with 185 g (6½ oz) of the sugar in a large stainless steel bowl. Add the salt and the yeast and stir to combine, then make a well in the centre and add 1–1½ cups lukewarm water, adding the water carefully to form a thick batter (the amount of water will vary depending on the type of flour you are using). Cover the bowl with plastic wrap and leave in a warm place for 10 hours. The batter will almost double in size, and will then begin to shrink – this is when it needs to be fed. Lightly whisk the remaining flour and sugar to the batter, with enough lukewarm water, to make a thick batter again. Leave to sit again for 1 hour.

Encase a piece of mozzarella and one anchovy fillet between two squares of bread. Secure with a toothpick.

Preheat the oil to 180°C (350°F) in a deep-fryer or large heavy-based saucepan. Test the oil by dropping a little batter in it – if it sizzles furiously it is hot enough.

Dip each sandwich first into the milk, then into the batter to coat. Gently lower them into the hot oil and deep-fry, in batches, until golden. Drain on paper towel. Serve hot.

Pressed Octopus with Seaweed and Miso

Jim ⁓ Modern cookery is evolving constantly, and the barriers between cuisines and the traditional rules for what we can or cannot do seem to be dissolving. Chefs understand more about the science of food and the reactions between proteins and the ingredients used to prepare them. It is not a sin to use flavours or ideas from other cultures to enhance your own cooking style. It is a sin *not* to embrace as many cooking techniques and exotic ingredients as possible. This reinvention of Italian poached octopus is the product of my ongoing affection for Japanese cuisine.

Serves 10–15

4 sheets nori (dried seaweed)
750 ml (250 fl oz) sweet wine, such as
    moscato
1 large handful thyme
1 bulb garlic, cut in half crosswise
1 lemon, cut in half
50 g (1¾ oz) salt
1 medium-sized octopus
15 sheets gold-strength leaf gelatine,
    soaked in cold water until soft
baby shoots or frisée lettuce, to garnish

Miso Sauce
100 g (3½ oz) white miso paste
50 g (1¾ oz) unsalted butter, roughly
    chopped
juice of ½ lemon
salt and freshly ground black pepper

Line a 15 cm × 30 cm (6 inch x 12 inch) terrine tin or mould with plastic wrap. Place 2 of the nori sheets into the base the lined tin – they should overhang two sides of the tin.

Put the wine, thyme, garlic, lemon and salt into a large saucepan over high heat and bring to the boil.

Using a sharp knife, remove the tentacles from the octopus and discard the head. Place the octopus in the boiling stock, reduce the heat to medium, cover, and simmer for 15 minutes. Reduce the heat to low and leave the octopus to braise and steam for about 1 hour. You may need to add some chicken stock or water to the pan if the liquid gets too low.

When the octopus is tender, remove using a slotted spoon and transfer to the terrine mould. Transfer ½ cup (125 ml/4 fl oz) of the cooking liquid to a small saucepan over low heat. Add the softened gelatine sheets and stir until dissolved. Strain this mixture through a fine sieve into the terrine mould over the octopus.

Cut the remaining nori sheets to size so they fit the top of the tin. Place a similar-sized terrine tin on top with a weight in it (food tins work well for this) and refrigerate for at least 3 hours, or overnight to allow the octopus to set.

To make the Miso Sauce, place 100 ml (3½ fl oz) in a small saucepan and bring to the boil. Stir in the miso paste, reduce the heat to medium and simmer for about 5 minutes. Remove from the heat and whisk in the butter. Add the lemon juice and season with salt and pepper. Keep warm until ready to serve.

To serve, cut the terrine into 2 cm (¾ inch) slices and place on serving plates. Drizzle with the miso sauce and garnish with the frisée lettuce.

Stefano ⁓ *Octopus is ideal for making a quick summer salad. Simply poach the octopus as in the recipe opposite, then leave it to cool. Mix in a salad bowl 3 large octopus tentacles, sliced on an angle, the chopped heart of 1 celery stick (white part only), 1 cup cooked chickpeas (tinned is fine, rinse well), 1 finely chopped garlic clove, a little chopped flat-leaf (Italian) parsley and a dressing of extra-virgin olive oil, lemon juice and salt. Or, in the absence of chickpeas, cook some diced potatoes, carrots and celery separately and toss the octopus with these and a few cubes of avocado. Also dress with oil, salt, pepper and lemon, and some mayonnaise on the side.*

Crudo of Tuna with Frozen White Balsamic, Cucumber, Finger Lime and Caviar

This recipe is simple and quick to prepare. The best cut to use is the large loin of yellowfin tuna; kingfish is also a great substitute. The best caviar to use is Sterling or Tsar Nicola caviar, which can be purchased in jars. A good alternative is salmon or tuna roe.

Serves 4

2 cups (500 ml/17 fl oz) white balsamic vinegar

⅓ cup (80 g/2¾ oz) caster (superfine) sugar

2 kg (4 lb 8 oz) crushed ice

400 g (14 oz) skinless, boneless tuna loin, sliced into 2 cm (¾ inch) cubes using a very sharp knife

4 native finger limes or use orange segments, white pith removed

1 continental (telegraph) cucumber, peeled, seeded and diced into 5 mm (¼ inch) cubes

30 g (1 oz) caviar

1 punnet baby shiso or other peppery cress

extra-virgin olive oil, for drizzling

Gently heat the vinegar and sugar in a saucepan over medium heat, stirring to dissolve the sugar. Taste for balance – it should not be sweet; the sugar should counteract the acid in the vinegar but not take it away completely. Pour into a tray and freeze for 1–2 hours, or until solid.

Place four dinner plates in the freezer to chill for 30 minutes before serving. Place the crushed ice in a baking tray and wrap with plastic wrap. Don't wrap too tightly, as you want the plastic wrap touching the ice. Lay the tuna on the plastic wrap over the ice to keep it cold.

Halve the finger limes and, using a teaspoon, gently spoon out the pearls of fruit and place in a bowl. If using orange segments, break the flesh into small pieces.

Remove the frozen balsamic mixture from the freezer and roughly scrape the surface using a fork. The balsamic should resemble fine snow – if not, return to the freezer for a further 30 minutes. Pour the balsamic snow into a container as you make it and return to the freezer. Scrape as much ice off the balsamic as you can, and when it starts to melt return it to the freezer to set. Continue this process until you have enough snow to scatter over the serving plates.

Arrange the tuna on the chilled plates. Scatter with the cucumber and finger lime pearls, and spoon over as much frozen white balsamic as you wish, about 1½ tablespoons per plate. Garnish with caviar, baby shiso and a nice drizzle of olive oil.

Stefano ⌣ Ah! This is where crudo, which is meant to be just that – crude – goes out of control. And yet, there are two classic Italians here: white balsamic and extra-virgin olive oil. This is really where typical Italian ideas are developed to a crazy point, and antipasto pushes new boundaries! Bravo, Jim!

Lamb Sweetbread Nuggets with Pickled Onion Mayonnaise

Jim 〜 I have nightmarish memories of learning how to perfectly pan-fry lamb sweetbreads. My chef used to always say, 'When they are perfect they should look like chicken nuggets'. That has obviously stayed with me because here it is, the realisation of the perfect sweetbread – a nugget! I wish I could have produced what my chef wanted with as little hassle and skill as it takes to produce this recipe. If you are not game to try this with lamb sweetbreads, cubes of flathead fillets work well.

Serves 4

vegetable oil, for deep-frying
16 small lamb sweetbreads
plain (all-purpose) flour, for dusting
200 g (7 oz) Pickled Onion Mayonnaise
(page 188)

Batter
100 g (3½ oz) rice flour
⅔ cup (100 g/3½ oz) plain (all-purpose) flour
1 tablespoon finely chopped rosemary
1 teaspoon ground cumin
2 cups (500 ml/17 fl oz) iced water

To make the Batter, combine the rice and plain flours, rosemary and cumin in a large bowl. Add the iced water and roughly mix to combine (lumpy is fine).

Preheat the oil to 180°C (350°F) in a deep-fryer or large heavy-based saucepan. Test the oil by dropping a little batter in it – if it sizzles furiously it is hot enough.

Toss the sweetbreads first in the flour, then drop in the batter to coat. Deep-fry the sweetbreads, in batches, until golden brown. Drain well on paper towel and serve with the Pickled Onion Mayonnaise for dipping.

Stefano 〜 *I really enjoy this recipe made with vegetables such as cauliflower, broccoli and zucchini batons. If the vegetables need pre-cooking, like cauliflower for example, cook in plenty of lightly salted water and cool in a cold water bath before flouring and battering as above. If you wish, make a simple mayonnaise, but the addition of the onions is really nice.*

Carne Cruda with Black Truffle and Egg Yolk Cooked in Oil

Carne cruda is the Italian name for diced raw meat; the French call it steak tartare. Although it is a similar concept, the differences between the two dishes are quite significant. Italians tend to limit the additions to lemon, olive oil, salt and pepper, and sometimes truffles. The French add things like vinegar, and Tabasco and tomato sauces. This version is somewhere in between. This recipe also works well with an oily fish like tuna, kingfish or salmon. If you can't find a truffle, finish the dish with a drizzle of truffle oil.

Preheat the oven to 180°C (350°F/Gas 4).

Cut the baguette on an angle into 3 mm (⅛ inch) slices. If the bread is too fresh, place it in the freezer until it is firm so you can get a good clean slice. Toast in the oven for about 10 minutes, or until crisp but not rock hard.

Cut the beef into 5 mm (¼ inch) cubes. You can use a mincer if you wish, but hand-cutting using a very sharp knife gives a superior texture. Refrigerate until required.

Pour the olive oil into a small shallow tray (a tray is best because it is easier to remove the eggs when they are done) and set over medium heat until the oil reaches about 60°C (140°F). The oil should not be hot enough to make the eggs go white or sizzle. Gently lower the yolks into the oil and cook for 25–30 minutes. Drain on paper towel.

Meanwhile, add the parsley, capers, shallots, Mayonnaise and lemon juice to the beef. Season with salt and pepper and stir to combine.

Divide the beef between four chilled serving plates. Arrange into mounds and use a spoon to make an indentation in the top of each, large enough to cradle the egg yolk. Set the yolks into the hollow, and season. Liberally grate the truffle over each portion.

Serve with the toasted baguette slices on the side.

Serves 4

1 baguette
400 g (14 oz) beef eye fillet or similar lean meat, trimmed of sinew
4 cups (1 litre/35 fl oz) olive oil (any leftover oil can be strained and reused)
4–6 free-range egg yolks (you may need extra in case of breakage)
1 tablespoon chopped flat-leaf (Italian) parsley
1 teaspoon capers, rinsed, drained and chopped
1 French shallot, finely chopped
1 tablespoon Mayonnaise (page 188)
juice of ½ lemon
salt and freshly ground black pepper
15–20 g (½–¾ oz) black truffle

Baccalà with Smoked Murray Cod

Jim ⌣ This recipe consists of two preparations of cod. The first is Murray cod that has been cured and smoked, similar to smoked salmon; the second is the classic Italian *baccalà mantecato* or creamed cod. Each is lovely on its own but together they are outstanding. You will need to soak the salt cod over a three-day period, changing the water several times during this time. Or look for shops that sell a desalinated fish.

Serves about 5

150 g (5½ oz) Murray cod, blue-eye trevalla
    or any other firm white fish, deboned and
    filleted
150 g (5½ oz) Basic Cure
    (page 184)
100 g (3½ oz) wood smoking chips
grilled slices of sourdough bread, to serve
capers, to garnish
extra-virgin olive oil, for drizzling

Baccalà
500 g (1 lb 2 oz) salt cod, washed
400 ml (14 fl oz) full-cream (whole) milk
1 bay leaf
1 sprig thyme
4 whole black peppercorns
1 boiled potato, peeled
100 ml (3½ fl oz) pouring (whipping) cream
juice of ½ lemon
1 clove garlic, crushed
1 tablespoon extra-virgin olive oil
salt

Put some of the Basic Cure mixture in a bowl with the fish on top. Cover the fish with the remaining cure and press the mixture around the fish to ensure it is well covered. Refrigerate for 8 hours.

Put the smoking chips in a deep roasting tray. Place the cod in a perforated baking tray that will fit inside the roasting tray with the chips. Stack the trays, cover with foil and place over high heat until the chips are smoking furiously. You can use a stovetop but this may smoke out your house, so an outdoor barbecue with a lid is the best option. Turn off the heat and leave for 20 minutes for the smoke to infuse. Turn the cod over and repeat this smoking step three or four times until the cod smells very smoky.

To make the Baccalà, put the salt cod, milk, bay leaf, thyme and peppercorns into a large saucepan and bring to the boil, then reduce the heat to low and poach the cod for 15 minutes, or until the cod is tender. Strain and reserve the milk, discarding the peppercorns, thyme and bay leaves. Leave the cod to cool slightly, then squeeze out any extra moisture. Place the cod in the bowl of an electric mixer fitted with a paddle attachment. Mix on low speed until the cod has broken down. Add the potato, cream, lemon juice, garlic and 2 tablespoons of the reserved milk. Continue to blend, adding the oil in a slow, steady stream. Taste and season with salt and more lemon juice, milk or oil, if needed.

Serve the baccalà in quenelles on the bread with a few slices of the smoked cod arranged on tip. Garnish with capers and drizzle with olive oil.

Grilled Ox Tongue, Bone Marrow Toast and Salsa Verde

Jim ⌒ Ox tongue was something I experienced when I was an apprentice in Stefano's restaurant and it remains one of my favourite things to cook. I learnt in other restaurants how to prepare it in many amazing ways: pickled and poached, in a terrine or grilled. This dish uses two of Stefano's simple recipes: salsa verde and grilled tongue. I have added a simple bone marrow toast. Hot-smoked tongue can be found at most good butchers' shops.

Serves 4–6

80 g (2¾ oz) bone marrow centres
50 g (1¾ oz) unsalted butter
200 g (7 oz) hot-smoked ox tongue, cut
    into 5 mm (¼ inch) slices
salt flakes

Ciabatta Croutons
1 ciabatta loaf
olive oil, for drizzling
1 clove garlic, cut in half

Salsa Verde
3 free-range eggs
1 bunch flat-leaf (Italian) parsley, finely
    chopped
½ bunch basil, finely chopped
1 tablespoon lilliput capers, rinsed,
    drained and finely chopped
5 cornichons (pickled baby cucumbers),
    finely chopped
juice of 1 small lemon
2 tablespoons grated Parmigiano
    Reggiano cheese
100 ml (3½ fl oz) olive oil
salt and freshly ground black pepper

Preheat the oven to 180°C (350°F/Gas 4).

To make the Ciabatta Croutons, cut the bread on an angle into 1 cm (½ inch) slices. If the bread is too fresh, place it in the freezer until it is firm so you can get a good clean slice. Drizzle the bread with a little olive oil and then toast in the oven for about 10 minutes, or until crisp but not rock hard. Rub half the garlic clove sparingly around the edges of each bread slice.

To make the Salsa Verde, place the eggs in a saucepan of cold water, bring to the boil and simmer for 6 minutes, or until hard-boiled. Remove the eggs from the pan, allow to cool slightly, then peel off and discard the shell and chop the egg. Transfer to a bowl and add all of the remaining ingredients. Stir to combine and season with salt and pepper. Refrigerate until ready to serve.

Put the bone marrow and butter in a small saucepan and cook over low heat until the marrow becomes soft – it does not have to be a fine purée, as long as the marrow is soft it will spread. Set aside and keep warm.

Heat a grill pan over high heat until smoking. Place the tongue in the pan and cook for about 30 seconds on each side.

To serve, spread the marrow butter over the ciabatta croutons. Season with salt flakes. Place the grilled tongue on warm serving plates, put the toast on the side and garnish with a nice dollop of salsa verde. Alternatively, if you want to present it as refined finger food, arrange the tongue on each piece of toast and top with the salsa verde.

Stefano ⁓ *I have two comments here: as a traditionalist I still prefer a brined ox tongue, that is, a tongue that has been cured with salt and has turned a lovely pink colour. All butchers are familiar with this and it is easy to procure anywhere. It follows that it must be poached in water with the addition of root vegetables and a couple of aromatic cloves and bay leaves. This takes about two or three hours, depending on size. It is exceptional straight out of the pot, sliced still hot, and served with Salsa Verde. Or, peel when cold, slice and grill, making sure the grill pan has been lightly oiled or the tongue will stick.*

I am also opposed to using the food processor for Salsa Verde, as most blades are never sharp enough. I prefer to chop with a sharp knife. I also like the addition of a couple of chopped fillets of anchovies to make the salsa verde more robust. You can also thicken the salsa with some bread: soften it first with a little stock from the tongue's poaching liquid. Use good-quality, two-day-old bread, crusts removed.

salads

Jim~

The role of the humble salad within a menu is a varied one. Salad can be served as part of a dish, as a side or even main course; the key to a memorable salad is balance and freshness. Many components work together to make the perfect salad, including acid, oil, crunch, sweet, salty and sour. The only real limitation when it comes to preparing a salad is imagination.

Stefano ~

The following recipes are hardly conventional salads. They are not just an assembly of fine leaves, although they do often contain greens, olive oil and lemons.

This section is almost entirely Jim's. Here, many traditional Italian elements, such as tomatoes, asparagus, ricotta and anchovies have been thrown around with complete abandon: no rules, no clear boundaries; Jim is guided by intuition. Look out for the method for cooking asparagus in the Salad of Asparagus with Quail Egg, Parmesan Velouté and Pancetta on page 54: it's a good one to learn.

Fruit and Vegetable Salad with Rockmelon and Chilli Dressing

This is a vegetarian, vegan and gluten-free dish. The heat of the chilli and the sweetness of the other ingredients make this salad a perfect match with a pale ale that displays citrus and tropical characters. It was developed with visiting Italian chef Marco Paladini, for Stefano's Storm Pale Ale.

Using a vegetable peeler, shave three strips each from the zucchini and carrot (this recipe is for a single serve and so only uses part of the zucchini and carrot; scale as required to make multiple serves). Warm the olive oil in a frying pan over low heat and add the zucchini and carrot shavings. Cook gently just long enough for them to wilt, then remove from the heat.

Make the Sauce by blending the rockmelon, spring onion and chilli powder together in a blender or food processor. Add some olive oil, lemon juice, salt and pepper. Make it as tasty and as aggressive as you like.

Arrange the zucchini and carrot with the remaining fruit and vegetables on a serving plate, starting with the wilted vegetables as the base of the composition.

Dress generously with the rockmelon sauce. If you like, add more extra-virgin olive oil, and season with salt and pepper.

Serves 1, so multiply as required

1 zucchini (courgette)
1 carrot
1 tablespoon extra-virgin olive oil, plus extra
    for drizzling
6 small lettuce leaves
2 wedges ripe tomato, skinned and seeded
1 strawberry, cut in half or as desired
2 raspberries
1 radish, cut into thin matchsticks and kept
    in chilled water
1 small piece fennel, finely sliced and kept
    in chilled water
3 slices pear, kept in acidulated water
3 slices apple, kept in acidulated water
1 tablespoon pomegranate seeds
salt and freshly ground black pepper

Sauce
1 large slice rockmelon, skinned
1 spring onion (scallion), white part only
a pinch of hot chilli powder, or more to taste
extra-virgin olive oil, for blending
1 tablespoon lemon juice, or to taste
salt and freshly ground black pepper

Salad of Beetroot, Goat's Cheese, Apple and Blood Orange

These ingredients are a textbook match in anyone's language; the acidic sweetness of the goat's cheese and apple perfectly complement the beetroot. Cider vinegar works in the dressing because of the link with the apple. We prefer to cook the beetroot in cheap white vinegar, liking the hit of harsh acidity it gives the beetroot. Use this method every time you cook beetroot and no matter what the dish, it will be terrific.

Serves 4

2 large beetroot (beets)

1½ tablespoons caster (superfine) sugar

200 ml (7 fl oz) white vinegar, plus extra if necessary

1½ tablespoons table salt

1 tablespoon capers, rinsed and drained

½ red onion, finely chopped

1 tablespoon chopped cornichons (pickled baby cucumbers)

salt and freshly ground black pepper

a good handful of baby rocket (arugula)

1 large apple

2 tablespoons cider vinegar

5 tablespoons extra-virgin olive oil

2 blood oranges

250 g (9 oz) goat's cheese

Place the beetroot, sugar, vinegar and salt in a saucepan with 4 cups (1 litre/35 fl oz) water over high heat. Bring to the boil, then reduce the heat to low and simmer until the beetroot are tender but still a little firm when a knife is inserted into them. Remove from the heat and allow the beetroot to cool in their cooking juices. When cool, peel the beetroot and chop into 2 cm (¾ inch) dice.

Place the beetroot in a bowl with the capers, onion and cornichons. Season with salt, pepper and a splash of vinegar if needed (the cooking liquor should add a bit of acidity to your beetroot but sometimes a splash of vinegar is needed).

Place the baby rocket in a separate bowl and coarsely grate the apple into the bowl and combine. Add the balsamic vinegar and olive oil.

Using a small paring knife, cut the skin off one blood orange, remove the segments and squeeze out all the juice from the leftover pith. Juice the second orange and place in a jug or bowl with the segmented orange.

Divide the beetroot mixture between serving bowls. Top with the rocket and apple salad and dress with the blood orange segments and juice. Crumble the goat's cheese over the top and serve.

Salad of Prawn and Sweet Corn with Burghul

Think of this as Italian-influenced couscous. It sounds like a strange combination but it works. It's fun to prepare and makes a great summer salad. Burghul is delicious, and is an excellent addition to a salad to add texture and substance.

Place the burghul in a bowl (remember it will double in volume as it soaks) and pour over the boiling salted water. Cover the bowl tightly with plastic wrap and leave in a warm place for 20 minutes.

After 20 minutes, unwrap the bowl and stir in the butter, corn, onions, parsley and most of the lemon juice. Use a fork to mix well and aerate the burghul.

Dress the prawns with the oil, lemon juice and salt.

Spoon the burghul onto serving plates and top with the prawns. Garnish with watercress.

Serves 4

200 g (7 oz) burghul (bulgur)

200 ml (7 fl oz) boiling salted water

1 tablespoon unsalted butter, at room temperature

2 cobs sweet corn, kernels removed

1 tablespoon finely chopped red onion

1 tablespoon finely chopped flat-leaf (Italian) parsley

juice of 1 lemon

16 cooked prawns (shrimp), peeled and deveined

1/3 cup (80 ml/2½ fl oz) extra-virgin olive oil

salt

watercress, for garnish

Salad of Tomato, White Anchovy, Basil, Olive and Onion

It may sounds obvious, but the best advice we can give you when using tomatoes is to make sure they are red and ripe. Green or unripe varieties have their culinary uses but they are not welcome in this recipe. This is a dish designed to be shared on a large plate or platter and is built in layers.

Serves 4–6 as a shared plate

5 large pitted kalamata olives or other good black olives
100 ml (3½ fl oz) white vinegar
1 tablespoon caster (superfine) sugar
1 red onion, cut into 5 mm (¼ inch) thick rings
1 tablespoon salt flakes
4 large round tomatoes, cut into 1 cm (½ inch) thick slices
salt and freshly ground black pepper
100 ml (3½ fl oz) extra-virgin olive oil
6 white anchovy fillets, halved crosswise
1 small handful fresh basil leaves

Place the olives in the freezer.

Combine the vinegar and sugar in a saucepan, place over medium heat and stir until the sugar has dissolved. Remove from the heat and allow to cool slightly.

Reserve the small inner and large outer onion rings for another use. For this recipe, we'll use only the even, medium-sized onion rings. Place them in a bowl with the salt. Leave for a few minutes to soften a little. Pour over the vinegar mixture and set aside.

Arrange the tomatoes on a large serving plate. Season with salt and pepper, then drizzle with the olive oil. Arrange the anchovy fillets over the top, spacing them evenly to ensure that each diner gets at least one.

Remove the olives from the freezer and grate them over the tomato and anchovy. Use as much or as little as you like.

Scatter the onion rings over the top. The salad should be gaining some height and interest by now. Garnish with the basil leaves.

Jim ~ Stinging nettles grow wild in Australia and are treated as a serious weed. They are extremely painful when they come into contact with the skin, so wear gloves when handling them. After the nettle is cooked the taste is unique and its stinging properties disappear. If nettles are out of season or hard to come by in your part of the world, you can use wild rocket, silverbeet or spinach to make my salad (page 50).

Duck

Stefano ～ Jim's salad is terrific. However, it leaves you with quite a bit of duck fat. That's no problem because you can use it again and again for the same recipe or to cook such things as potatoes. My recipe (page 51) is quick and easy and has no leftovers. It makes an ideal warm starter to a meal in the cooler months.

Jim's Warm Potato and Stinging Nettle Salad with Shredded Duck

Serves 4–6

4 duck legs

salt and freshly ground black pepper

3 sprigs thyme

4 cups (1 litre/35 fl oz) olive oil or
    duck fat

20–30 small fingerling or chat
    potatoes, unpeeled

100 ml (3½ fl oz) extra-virgin
    olive oil

4 cloves garlic, chopped

5 anchovy fillets, chopped

80 g (2¾ oz) unsalted butter

3 bunches small stinging nettles
    (see note, page 48)

2 French shallots, chopped

3 tablespoons capers, rinsed,
    drained and chopped

3 tablespoons snipped chives

1¼ cups (300 g/10½ oz)
    Mayonnaise (page 188)

1 tablespoon white vinegar

wild rocket (arugula) or mizuna, to
    garnish

Preheat the oven to 120°C (235°F/Gas ½).

Season the duck legs well with salt and pepper and place in a baking tray or a small saucepan. Add the thyme and cover with the olive oil or duck fat. Cover with foil and cook in the oven for 3–4 hours, or until the flesh is very soft. (The duck can be stored in the fat for weeks.) Remove the duck from the fat and leave at room temperature for 10–15 minutes. Shred the meat, discarding the bones, and set aside (do not refrigerate or the fat will set).

Bring a large saucepan of salted water to the boil. Add the potatoes and cook for about 12–15 minutes, or until cooked through but still firm. Strain, and when cool enough to handle, peel the potatoes, set aside and keep warm.

Heat a little olive oil in a frying pan over low heat. Add the garlic and anchovies and cook until softened without colour. Add the potatoes and butter and cook for a further 3 minutes, or until the potatoes start to colour. When the potatoes are nicely browned add the nettle leaves and toss until they start to wilt. Remove from the heat and allow to cool for 5–10 minutes.

In a small bowl, combine the shallots, capers, chives and Mayonnaise, and season to taste. Add to the potato mixture with the vinegar, and stir well to coat.

Arrange the dressed potatoes in a serving bowl and scatter the shredded duck over the top. Garnish with rocket, to serve.

Stefano's Warm Salad of Duck

Serves 1

1 plump duck breast
salt and freshly ground black pepper
1 tablespoon olive oil
1 tablespoon good-quality balsamic
    vinegar
mixed fresh salad leaves, to serve
salt and freshly ground black pepper
mustard fruits, to garnish

Preheat the oven to 180°C (350°F/Gas 4).

Trim a bit less than half the fat and skin from the duck breast. With a sharp knife, make some incisions in the skin. Season lightly with salt and pepper.

Heat the olive oil in an ovenproof frying pan over high heat. Add the duck, skin side down, and cook until the skin turns dark brown. Turn over and continue cooking for a couple of minutes. Turn the breast back over, transfer to the oven and cook for a further 7–9 minutes, depending on its size – press on the breast to see if it is firm. If not, firm, return to the oven for a few minutes, but be careful to not overcook it. Remove from the oven and rest for a couple of minutes. Once the pan has cooled, add the balsamic vinegar to the rendered duck fat and rest for a further 5 minutes.

Arrange the salad leaves on a serving plate. Cut the duck breast in slices across the grain to maximise tenderness, collecting the juices and returning them to the pan. Arrange the duck on the salad.

Return the pan to the heat to warm and emulsify the liquid. Stir until the juices and the vinegar are well combined. Pour over the duck, season with salt and pepper, and garnish with mustard fruits, to serve.

Grilled Peach, Warm Buffalo Mozzarella and Prosciutto

This dish is about as easy to prepare as it gets, but relies completely on the quality of the ingredients. If the ingredients you source are the best available, the dish will sing. If peaches are not in season, rockmelon is a good substitute, but it's best to wait until peaches are at their peak.

Preheat a grill pan until it is smoking hot.

Stand a peach up on a chopping board with the stem end facing up and slice off the cheeks. (There will be a bit of wastage but you can dice the remaining flesh and sprinkle over the salad, or just eat it on the spot.) Repeat for each peach.

Rub a little olive oil onto the cut surface of each peach cheek and grill for about 20 seconds on each side, or until there are lovely grill marks on the peach.

Heat the olive oil in a small saucepan over low heat for about 5 minutes. Add the mozzarella and continue to heat for a further 2 minutes. Remove from the heat and let it sit so the mozzarella warms through.

Arrange the grilled peach on serving plates. Remove the mozzarella from the oil and arrange a few pieces on each plate. Place the prosciutto on top – the prosciutto lets you give height to the dish when plating, so be creative. Garnish with rocket and spoon some of the warm oil over the salad. This dish is best eaten with some good crusty bread.

Serves 4

4 firm peaches
300 ml (10½ fl oz) extra-virgin olive oil
4 small or 2 large buffalo mozzarella, torn into bite-sized pieces
16 thin slices prosciutto
wild rocket (arugula), to garnish
crusty bread, to serve

Salad of Asparagus with Quail Egg, Parmesan Velouté and Pancetta

In Mildura we get asparagus that is world class, and at the height of its season it is our favourite vegetable. The cooking method is unconventional, but once mastered, it will be your benchmark for cooking asparagus. This method uses both pressure-cooking and steaming to cook the asparagus in about twenty seconds. If you are uncomfortable attempting this technique, just boil the asparagus in salted water.

Serves 4

500 g (1 lb 2 oz) ice

16 spears asparagus, trimmed

a large pinch of salt

50 ml (1¾ fl oz) vegetable oil

8 slices pancetta, about 2 mm (1/16 inch) thick

1 loaf brioche or regular white bread, torn into small pieces

100 g (3½ oz) butter, melted

8 cooked quail eggs (page 187), peeled and halved lengthwise

Parmesan Velouté

2 cups (500 ml/17 fl oz) Chicken Stock (page 191)

4 sprigs thyme

2 cloves garlic, bruised

2 cups (500 ml/17 fl oz) UHT milk

2 cups (200 g/7 oz) grated Parmigiano Reggiano cheese

1 sheet of titanium-strength leaf gelatine, soaked in cold water until soft

a pinch of salt flakes

Mix the ice with some water to prepare an ice bath – reserve about 10 ice cubes and place in a bowl with the asparagus. Season the asparagus liberally with salt.

Heat the vegetable oil in a heavy-based saucepan until smoking. Hold the saucepan lid in one hand and the asparagus in the other. Quickly throw the asparagus and ice into the pan; the oil will spit, so cover with the lid immediately. Hold the lid down tightly and shake the pan every few seconds – after about 20 seconds the asparagus should be cooked. Pour the entire contents into the ice bath and chill. The asparagus will look raw and super green, but will be beautifully *al dente*. Set aside, unrefrigerated, until needed.

Preheat the oven to 160°C (320°F/Gas 2–3).

Place the pancetta on a tray lined with baking paper and place a similar-sized tray on top. Bake for 25–30 minutes, or until crisp and brown. Remove from the oven and set aside.

Place the brioche pieces on a baking tray and brush with the melted butter to coat. Roast in the oven for 10 minutes, or until lightly browned. Remove from the oven and set aside to cool.

To make the Parmesan Velouté, put the stock in a saucepan over high heat. Add the thyme and garlic and simmer until the stock has reduced to about 150 ml (5 fl oz). Strain into a clean saucepan, discarding the thyme and garlic. Add the milk, place over high heat and bring to the boil. Remove from the heat and stir in the cheese. Remove the gelatine from its soaking water. Squeeze out excess water and stir into the milk until dissolved. Use a hand-held stick blender to combine well. Season with salt, and keep warm over low heat.

When you are ready to serve, divide the asparagus between serving plates and arrange the quail eggs on top. Garnish with the pancetta.

Heat the velouté until it is almost boiling. Blend the mixture again using a hand-held stick blender until light and frothy. Spoon the froth, and then some of the velouté, generously over the salad. Garnish with the roasted bread.

Pea, Broad Bean and Ricotta Salad

Jim ⁓ I originally created this dish using vetch leaves. Vetch is a type of
pea that grows wild in Mildura during winter and spring. This recipe calls for
watercress as it is more readily available. The peppery flavour of the watercress
is a wonderful complement to the lemon and ricotta.

Serves 4

200 g (7 oz) fresh ricotta
1 small French shallot, finely diced
1 clove garlic, crushed
finely grated zest of ½ lemon
juice of ½ lemon
80 ml (2½ fl oz) extra-virgin olive oil
salt flakes and freshly ground black pepper
⅔ cup (100 g/3½ oz) fresh broad (fava)
    beans, podded
¾ cup (100 g/3½ oz) fresh peas, podded
4 egg yolks cooked in oil (see page 33)
about 10 sprigs watercress, wild vetch
    shoots or chickpea shoots

Rocket Dressing
50 g (1¾ oz) rocket (arugula)
⅓ cup (80 ml/2½ fl oz) extra-virgin olive oil
juice of 1 lemon

To make the Rocket Dressing, put the rocket in a blender or food
processor with 300 ml (10½ fl oz) water and blend or process until
quite fine. Strain and reserve the liquid, discarding any pulp. Add
the olive oil and lemon juice. Season with salt. There is no need for
pepper here as the rocket juice is already quite peppery.

In a bowl, combine the ricotta, shallot, half of the garlic, the lemon
zest and juice and 2½ tablespoons of the olive oil. Season with salt
and pepper. Set aside.

Cover the broad beans with boiling water and allow to steep for
about 2 minutes – this will soften the skins but leave the broad
beans relatively raw. Strain and rinse under cold running water for
20 seconds or so. Peel the beans and add to a clean saucepan with
the peas and the remaining crushed garlic. Set over low heat and
add the remaining olive oil. Season with salt and gently warm; do
not allow them to fry.

To serve, place a 7 cm (2¾ inch) food ring on a serving plate and
spoon in the seasoned ricotta mixture to make a neat circle. Make
an indentation in the centre of the ricotta large enough to cradle an
egg yolk. Repeat on each plate. Scatter the warmed peas and beans
around the ricotta on each plate, top with the egg yolks and season
with salt and pepper. Garnish with the watercress.

Flood the plates with the rocket dressing at the table for a bit of fun.

Salad of Yabby, Baby Cos, Nashi and Caramelised Macadamias

Yabbies, the small freshwater crustaceans abundant in Mildura and much of Australia, are the star of this recipe. If you cannot get hold of yabbies, you can use saltwater crayfish, marron or prawns (shrimp). We make an oil with the yabby shells, which is used in the dressing; this technique can be applied to almost all crustaceans.

Serves 4

12 large raw yabbies (freshwater crayfish)
1 kg (2 lb 4 oz) ice
200 ml (7 fl oz) Yabby Oil (page 189)
100 ml (3½ fl oz) blood orange juice
salt
2 heads baby cos (romaine), washed and
    leaves separated
1 nashi pear, peeled, cored and cut into
    5 cm (2 inch) long batons
12 fennel fronds (or use dill fronds)

Caramelised Macadamias
100 g (3½ oz) caster (superfine) sugar
20 macadamia nuts
vegetable oil, for deep-frying

Place the yabbies in the freezer for 30 minutes. This makes them docile and slows their metabolism, and humanely despatches them. Combine the ice with 1 litre (35 fl oz) of water in a large bowl to make an ice bath.

Place a large saucepan of heavily salted water over high heat (see Blanching, page 184). When cooking crustaceans, the water should taste like seawater. Remove the yabbies from the freezer. Using your finger, gently prise off the middle fin on the bottom of the tail. As you remove the fin, the intestinal tract should come with it. Repeat with all the yabbies. Drop the yabbies into the boiling water and cook for 5–6 minutes, depending on their size. Remove and immediately place in the ice bath to halt the cooking process. When cool, peel the yabbies. Reserve the shells for the Yabby Oil and refrigerate the meat.

To make the Caramelised Macadamias, put the oil in a deep-fryer or large heavy-based saucepan and heat the oil to 170°C (325°F). Test the oil by dropping a little bread in it – if it sizzles furiously it is hot enough. Lightly grease a baking tray and set aside.

Put the caster sugar and 2 tablespoons water in a saucepan over high heat and stir until the sugar has dissolved. Add the macadamias and cook for 3 minutes, then remove the nuts using a slotted spoon and spread them out on the oiled tray to cool. When the sugar has solidified and the nuts are cool enough to handle, gently lower them into the hot oil, in batches, and deep-fry until golden brown. Return to the oiled tray to cool. When the nuts are cool they should be very crisp.

Make a vinaigrette by whisking together the yabby oil and blood orange juice. Place the yabby tails and cos in a separate bowl and add enough of the dressing to generously coat. Season with salt. Arrange the cos and yabbies on serving plates. Garnish with the macadamias, nashi and wild fennel fronds. Spoon over any leftover dressing as desired.

Poached Lobster with Crab Coleslaw

More of a starter than a salad, this is a dish for a summer's day. It requires only a little preparation, after which it is quite easy to pull together. Start by sourcing the best crayfish you can; southern rock lobster is the most common and the best in Australia, but can be substituted with a freshwater marron or even a lovely piece of cod or monkfish. Avoid imported crayfish because the quality of most is vastly inferior. On the other hand, there are some very good frozen crab products available; the best is picked spanner crabmeat frozen in seawater, which can be sourced from any good fishmonger. You can barely tell the difference from fresh.

Place the lobster in the freezer for 30 minutes. This makes them docile and slows their metabolism, and humanely dispatches them.

Bring a large saucepan of water to the boil. Plunge the lobster into the water and turn off the heat. After 2 minutes, remove the lobster and remove the tail. Using scissors, cut away the under-cartilage of the tail and carefully remove the entire tail meat. Wrap the lobster tail in plastic wrap and roll into a cylinder. Return the meat to the water, still off the heat, for about 20 minutes. This gently poaches the lobster rather than boiling, so the tail meat will be beautifully tender. Slice the lobster tail into 4–6 medallions and refrigerate until ready to serve.

To make the Crab Coleslaw, combine all of the ingredients in a large bowl and use your hands to toss everything together. Season with salt and pepper, adding a little extra lemon juice, if desired. Set aside.

To make a sauce, juice all the fruit, reserving a few segments from each to roughly chop. Pour the sauce into a jug and stir in the olive oil, sugar, dill and vinegar. Add the chopped fruit.

To serve, divide the crab coleslaw between serving plates and balance two medallions of lobster on top. Season with some salt and drizzle with the sauce.

Serves 4–6

1 live medium-sized (about 1.2 kg/2 lb 10 oz) fresh southern rock lobster, or other crayfish
salt
2 oranges
1 lime
1 grapefruit
150 ml (5 fl oz) extra-virgin olive oil
1 teaspoon caster (superfine) sugar
1 tablespoon chopped dill
1 tablespoon white vinegar

Crab Coleslaw
300 g (10½ oz) crabmeat
1 small wombok (Chinese cabbage), finely shredded
5 spring onions (scallions), thinly sliced
1 small carrot, julienned
1 red onion, very thinly sliced
150 g (5½ oz) Mayonnaise (page 188)
2 tablespoons finely chopped flat-leaf (Italian) parsley
juice of ½ lemon
salt and freshly ground black pepper

soups & broths

Jim～

The satisfaction that can be gained from a puréed vegetable or an amazing roasted-meat broth teamed with something imaginative is immeasurable. Soups and broths have been a staple in peasant cooking since the dawn of humanity; more recently, the modern cook has taken this simple idea and evolved it into something full of wonder, excitement and mystery.

A simple broth is an incredibly effective vehicle for flavour. Mastered correctly, it can be one of the most valuable weapons in the cook's arsenal. The same techniques and rules apply to making a broth as they do to making a sauce – gelatine and body are the secrets to a good sauce or broth (with the exception of consommé, which should be a bit lighter). Good vegetables and spices are also important.

One of the keys to a good broth, puréed soup (or sauce) is the attention to its foundations: of first roasting the bones and vegetables, and most importantly, skimming off the impurities while the stock is cooking, and keeping the simmer very gentle. There is no point trying to make any kind of soup without an excellent stock. The more care you take when making a stock, the better it will be. Any burnt or bitter flavours will be magnified when the stock is finished.

Stefano~

In today's world, people buy ready-made stocks, which is fine for certain stocks, such as rich beef or veal reductions. Most of the time, a basic clean, flavoursome golden chicken stock will be all you need. The problem is that, in my experience, few people actually own a pot large enough for making stock and they have never learned how to make stock. So, read the recipes on pages 190–193, buy a large pot and start making stock. Once made, you can freeze it, and the rest will come easily.

Chilled Wild Sorrel Soup with Dressed Yabby and Celeriac

Wild sorrel is available abundantly in southern Australia, on roadsides or in green pastures, particularly during the spring. It is known to some as wood sorrel and is recognisable by its pretty yellow flowers, so remember the spot where you saw it and go back to it during the cooler months. This recipe is a simple adaptation of a chilled potato and leek soup. The sorrel adds an acidic freshness. If you can't find wild sorrel, use classic French sorrel.

To make the Wild Sorrel Soup, place a saucepan over medium heat and cook the onion, garlic and leek in the butter until the onion has softened. Add the potato, bay leaves, milk and stock, and simmer until the potato is tender, about 15 minutes. Remove from the heat, then transfer to a blender or food processor and blend or process on high speed until very smooth. Chill over an ice bath or in the refrigerator. When cold, add the spinach and sorrel and blend until smooth. Fold in the cream and season with salt and pepper.

Julienne one of the apples and combine with the celeriac, Mayonnaise, lemon juice and shallots. Add the yabbies and parsley and gently combine, then taste and adjust the seasoning as needed.

Cut the remaining apple into 1 cm (½ inch) cubes. Divide the chilled soup into bowls and top with the dressed yabbies, three per serve. Garnish with the apple and fennel fronds.

Serves 4

1½ Granny Smith apples
1 small celeriac, julienned
100 g (3½ oz) Mayonnaise (page 188)
juice of 1 lemon
2 French shallots, finely diced
12 cooked and peeled yabby (freshwater crayfish) tails (page 58)
2 tablespoons chopped flat-leaf (Italian) parsley
1 sprig fennel fronds (or use dill fronds)

Wild Sorrel Soup

½ onion, diced
5 cloves garlic, sliced
1 leek, chopped
¼ cup (60 g/2¼ oz) unsalted butter
3 potatoes, peeled and thinly sliced
3 bay leaves
2 cups (500 ml/17 fl oz) full-cream (whole) milk
700 ml (24 fl oz) Chicken Stock (page 191)
2 cups (90 g/3¼ oz) baby spinach leaves
1 cup (45 g/1¾ oz) wild sorrel leaves
100 ml (3½ fl oz) pouring (whipping) cream
salt and freshly ground black pepper

Duck Meatballs and Farfalle in Broth

The Duck Broth is best done overnight in the oven over a gentle heat; the stock will be clearer because it doesn't bubble. It can be done on the stovetop, but if you have the time and space, try cooking it in the oven. We have always found it better.

Serves 4

1 quantity Duck Broth (page 143)
2 cups (180 g/6½ oz) small farfalle pasta
    (farfalline)
1 good handful of grated Parmigiano
    Reggiano cheese, to serve
finely chopped flat-leaf (Italian) parsley,
    to garnish
extra-virgin olive oil, for drizzling

Meatballs
1 tablespoon duck fat or butter
½ small onion, finely diced
1 tablespoon finely diced pancetta
1 clove garlic, finely crushed
300 g (10½ oz) minced (ground) duck
100 g (3/½ oz) minced (ground) chicken
1 tablespoon chopped flat-leaf (Italian)
    parsley
1 tablespoon cornflour (cornstarch)
salt flakes and freshly ground black pepper

To make the Meatballs, heat the duck fat in a large saucepan over medium–high heat with the onion and pancetta until the pancetta is rendered and starting to crisp. Remove from the heat and stir in the garlic. Allow to stand for a few minutes.

Combine the minced duck and chicken in a large bowl with the parsley and cornflour. Add the onion mixture and use your hands to work everything together. Season with salt and pepper. You can fry off a little piece of the mixture to taste and adjust the seasonings accordingly. Take walnut-sized pieces of the mixture at a time and roll into balls. Refrigerate until ready to use.

Put the Duck Broth in a large saucepan and bring to the boil. Add the farfalle and the meatballs and simmer until the meatballs are cooked through and the pasta is *al dente* – keep checking to make sure the pasta is not overcooked.

Ladle the broth, farfalle and meatballs into serving bowls and garnish with cheese, parsley and good-quality olive oil.

Jerusalem Artichoke Soup with Flaked Salt Cod and Grilled Leek

When making soup it takes pretty much the same amount of time to make a large or small quantity. You can make less of this soup to serve fewer people than ten, but it keeps really well in the freezer for a quick mid-week meal.

Melt the butter and pork fat in a saucepan over medium heat. Add the onions, sage, garlic and oil and cook until the onion has softened but not coloured (otherwise it will turn the soup grey).

Add the artichoke, potato and stock, bring to the boil, then reduce the heat to low. Simmer for about 20 minutes, or until the artichoke is tender. Reserve about a quarter of the cooking liquid, and transfer the vegetables and remaining liquid to a blender or food processor. Blend or process the vegetables until very smooth, adding the reserved liquid as required to adjust to the desired consistency. Pour into a clean pan and stir in the cream, truffle oil and salt. Set aside in a warm place.

Flake the Salt Cod and set aside.

Preheat a heavy-based frying pan or grill pan until smoking hot. Add the leeks, cut-side down, and char for about 10 seconds. (If the leeks are thicker than a pencil, blanch in boiling water for 30 seconds before grilling.) Remove from the heat and slice each piece in half lengthwise.

Ladle the soup into bowls and top with the salt cod. Garnish with the leeks and drizzle with some good-quality olive oil.

Serves 10–15

50 g (1¾ oz) unsalted butter

1 tablespoon diced pork fat, lardo or pancetta (optional)

2 brown onions, peeled and chopped

10 sage leaves, stems discarded

1 head garlic, halved crosswise

50 ml (1¾ fl oz) vegetable oil or grapeseed oil

2 kg (4 lb 8 oz) Jerusalem artichokes, peeled and sliced

2 potatoes, peeled and sliced

8 cups (2 litres/70 fl oz) Chicken Stock (page 191)

100 ml (3½ fl oz) pouring (whipping) cream

1 teaspoon truffle oil

salt

500 g (1 lb 2 oz) cooked Salt Cod (page 156)

20–30 baby leeks, white part only

extra-virgin olive oil, for drizzling

Stefano~ *Salt cod, or baccalà, seems like an exotic fixation here in Australia. It is not until you visit places like Spain, Portugal and Italy that you realize what a magnificent and popular ingredient it is. Salt cod is readily available here in Australia and has the potential to become just as popular as other adopted Mediterranean ingredients. Many shops now offer baccalà desalinated and ready for use – making this once time-consuming ingredient more approachable for the home cook.*

Mushroom Consommé with Slow-roasted Baby Onions and Truffle Toasts

The darker the mushrooms, the better they are for the consommé. If you can't get dark mushrooms, just wrap the mushrooms with plastic wrap and leave in the pantry for a few days. There may be some consommé left over but it freezes well and we're willing to bet you will want to eat this one again.

Serves 4

1 large baguette, cut into 8 slices
150 g (5½ oz) Truffle Butter (page 186)
8 slices provolone
fresh shimeji mushrooms, to garnish
parsley shoots, to garnish (optional)
grated black truffle, to garnish (optional)

Mushroom Consommé

1 kg (2 lb 4 oz) field mushrooms,
    thinly sliced
100 g (3½ oz) dried porcini, soaked in
    hot water then drained
1 large handful thyme
1 bay leaf
finely grated zest of 1 lemon
200 ml (7 fl oz) port or madeira
4 cups (1 litre/35 fl oz) Chicken Stock or
    Vegetable Stock (both page 191)
soy sauce or salt and freshly ground black
    pepper, to taste

Slow-roasted Onions

12 baby onions, peeled
12 sprigs thyme
100 g (3½ oz) unsalted butter
1 cup (90 g/3¼ oz) fresh shimeji
    mushrooms
⅓ cup (80 ml/2½ fl oz) balsamic vinegar

To make the Mushroom Consommé, combine all of the ingredients, except for the soy sauce, in a large saucepan. Set over high heat and bring to the boil, then reduce the heat to low and simmer for 1 hour. Remove from the heat and strain into a clean saucepan – use a ladle to press on the solids to squeeze out all the juice. (This is very important because most of the colour comes from the mushrooms.) Taste and season with a dash of soy sauce, or with salt and pepper. A little bit of soy sauce is great for seasoning stocks; it adds a mild meaty flavour to this broth. Keep the stock hot until ready to use.

Preheat the oven to 160°C (315°F/Gas 2–3).

To make the Slow-roasted Onions, place the onions in a roasting tin and season with salt and pepper. Place a sprig of thyme on each onion with a small knob of butter. Roast for 30–40 minutes, or until the onions are tender and caramelised. Add the shimeji mushrooms and cook for a further 5 minutes. Remove from the oven, add the vinegar and toss to coat. Cut the onions in half and set aside.

Preheat a grill (broiler) to medium and toast the baguette on both sides. Spread the truffle butter on each slice and top with some provolone. Return to the grill and cook until the cheese has melted.

To serve, divide the onion between serving bowls and flood the plate with the consommé. Garnish with shimeji mushrooms, parsley shoots and grated truffle, if desired. Serve with the truffle toast on the side.

Stefano ～ My Quail Ravioli (page 76) has been the most popular dish in my restaurant for over twenty years. We have not taken it off the menu, partly because it is not commonly found in many other restaurants. There's not much point undertaking this dish, which is rather elaborate, for only a few serves – make enough for at least ten people and freeze what you do not need. The preparation time is rather long, especially if you are making it for the first time, but the cooking time is very short, making it an ideal fast-food.

Quail

Jim ～ I have designed my Quail and Cabbage Dumplings (page 77) using the influence of Stefano's famed quail ravioli, which is the absolute epitome of perfection and simplicity. Rather than try to recreate it I have done the opposite and made it a little more complicated – but equally rewarding. Once mastered, it is quite easy, but it may take a few attempts.

Stefano's Quail Ravioli

Serves 10

8 quail
4 cups (1 litre/35 fl oz) Chicken
    Stock (page 191)
100 g (3½ oz) unsalted butter
olive oil, for cooking
1 cup finely chopped carrots, celery
    and onions
1 free-range egg, plus 1 extra,
    lightly beaten
½ cup (70 g/2½ oz) grated
    Parmigiano Reggiano cheese,
    plus extra to serve
15 g (½ oz) fresh breadcrumbs
a little chopped flat-leaf (Italian)
    parsley
a little lemon zest
salt and freshly ground black pepper
300 g (10½ oz) Homemade Pasta
    (page 195)
plain (all-purpose) flour, for dusting
semolina, for dusting
100 g (3½ oz) salted butter
8 sage leaves

Separate the leg and breast meat from the quail. Put the skin and carcasses in a saucepan with enough Chicken Stock to cover, and simmer for 2 hours. Strain, discard solids and reduce to less than ½ cup (125 ml/4 fl oz). Set aside.

Heat the unsalted butter with some olive oil in a large frying pan over medium heat. Add the vegetables and cook until soft, then add the quail meat and cook for a few minutes until pink. Remove from the heat, transfer to a food processor and process to make a fine paste. Add one egg, cheese, breadcrumbs, parsley and lemon zest. Season and process to combine.

Roll the pasta through the thinnest setting of a pasta machine. Cut the sheet in half, and keep half under a clean damp tea towel to prevent it from drying out.

Place small dollops of quail filling at regular intervals in two rows along each sheet of pastry, about 4 cm (1½ inches) apart. Brush around the filling with the extra beaten egg. Place the other sheet of pasta neatly over the filling and gently press around the mounds to prevent air pockets. Cut with a ravioli cutter and place the ravioli on a tray dusted with a little flour and semolina. Cover with a clean tea towel and refrigerate until needed. You can freeze the ravioli at this point if you need.

Cook the ravioli in plenty of salted boiling water, making sure they are cooked around the edges. Melt the butter in a saucepan, add the sage leaves and when sizzling add a little of the quail stock. Swirl the pan around so the sauce emulsifies. Place the cooked ravioli in the sauce, and finish with extra cheese.

Jim's Quail and Cabbage Dumplings

Serves 4

4 quail, deboned (reserve the bones
    for the broth, see below)
½ chicken breast, trimmed of sinew,
    meat chopped
1 free-range egg
5 sage leaves, chopped
1 clove garlic, crushed
100 ml (3½ fl oz) pouring (whipping)
    cream
a good pinch of salt
4 wombok (Chinese cabbage) leaves,
    blanched and refreshed in
    ice water
4 quail eggs, lightly fried, to serve
extra-virgin olive oil, for drizzling

Quail Broth
reserved quail bones (see above)
1 carrot, chopped
2 French shallots, cut in half
2 sprigs thyme
2 cloves garlic, cut in half
1 stick celery, chopped
4 cups (1 litre/34 fl oz) Chicken
    Stock (page 191)

Preheat the oven to 180°C (350°F/Gas 4).

Remove and discard the skin from two of the quail and dice the flesh. Refrigerate until needed.

To make the Quail Broth, put the quail bones in a roasting tin and cook in the oven for 20 minutes, or until golden brown. Transfer the bones and all of the remaining ingredients to a large saucepan and bring to the boil. Reduce the heat to low and simmer for 2 hours. Strain and set aside. You will need to reheat before serving.

Put the chicken breast in a food processor and process for 1 minute. Scrape down the sides and repeat three times until very smooth. Add the egg and process for 15 seconds. Transfer to a mixing bowl, gently fold in the diced quail, sage, garlic, cream and salt. Spoon the mixture into a piping bag fitted with a 2 cm (¾ inch) nozzle and refrigerate until needed.

Cut the remaining quail in half lengthways (each piece should have breast and leg meat). Lay out four 25 cm (10 inch) squares of plastic wrap on a clean work surface. Cut the wombok leaves into 10–15 cm (4–6 inch) squares and place over the plastic wrap. Place a quail half on top of each and pipe about 2 tablespoons of the quail mixture in the middle. Wrap with the leaves to make parcels and tie the plastic wrap to enclose.

Cook the dumplings in a saucepan of hot, not boiling, water, for 15 minutes, or until firm to touch. To serve, ladle the quail broth into serving bowls. Unwrap the dumplings and place each in a bowl. Top with a fried quail egg, drizzle with olive oil and serve.

Minestrone with Crab

This is a flamboyant dish and can be complex to cook, but the result is fascinating and tasty. Tubetti rigati are short ribbed tubes of pasta, fantastic for soups – if unavailable, substitute any small pasta such as risoni or macaroni.

Serves 4 or more

4 whole blue-swimmer crabs
1 cup mixed chopped vegetables, such as
    carrots, celery, capsicum (pepper) and
    potatoes, cut into 5 mm (¼ inch) dice
olive oil, for cooking
1 tablespoon fennel seeds
1 dried chilli, chopped
1 large onion, roughly chopped
3 cloves garlic, crushed
1 stick celery, roughly chopped
1 bulb fennel, chopped
1 cup (250 ml/9 fl oz) white wine
1 cup (250 ml/9 fl oz) Napoli Sauce
    (page 194)
8 cups (2 litres/70 fl oz) Fish Stock
    (page 193)
½ cup (45 g/1½ oz) tubetti rigati
extra-virgin olive oil, for drizzling

Bring a saucepan of salted water to the boil. Add the crabs, cook for 6–8 minutes and then remove the crabs, reserving the cooking water. When cool, pick all the meat from the crabs, reserve the shells. Place the meat on a tray and gently go through it with your fingers to remove any shell or cartilage.

Add the vegetables to the saucepan of water and blanch them for about 2 minutes. Strain and set aside until needed.

Heat a little olive oil in a large saucepan over medium heat. Add the fennel seeds, chilli, onion, garlic, celery and fennel. Cook until soft, then add the wine – allow to evaporate, then add the Napoli Sauce. Finally, add the Fish Stock and the reserved crab shells (at this point, if you have them, you may also add prawn heads, pieces of fish, fish bones, etc. to add more flavour to the sauce). Stir to combine and allow to reduce a little. Remove from the heat and strain the soup through a fine
sieve – you should get a nice quantity of dark, rich, thick sauce. Season with salt and pepper, to taste, and keep warm.

Cook the tubetti rigati in a saucepan of salted boiling water according to the packet directions.

Divide the crab, diced vegetables and pasta between warm serving bowls. Ladle a sufficient amount of the sauce over to cover. Finish with a drizzle of extra-virgin olive oil. In daylight, this soup should look dazzling and taste very good. Leftover sauce is very good served simply with bread.

Thick Pea Soup with Poached Duck Egg, Pancetta and Witlof

This is more of a purée than a soup, but you can adjust the thickness as you wish. In the restaurant it is served as a first or second course so it is a small dish, but it can very easily be converted to a soup for lunch or dinner – just add more stock and double the soup recipe.

To make the Pea Soup, heat the butter in a saucepan over low heat. Add the onion and cook until they have softened but not coloured. Add 1 cup (250 ml/9 fl oz) of the stock and the peas, and bring to the boil. As soon as it boils, remove from the heat and transfer to a blender or food processor. Add the spinach, if using, and blend or process on high speed until smooth, adding more Chicken Stock if necessary. Stir in the remaining butter and season with salt and pepper. Set aside. You will need to reheat before serving.

To make the Dressing, heat the olive oil in a frying pan over medium heat. Add the pancetta and cook gently until the pancetta is golden brown and crisp. Add the garlic and cook for 1 minute, then add the lemon juice and stock. Bring to the boil briefly so all the cooking residue comes off the base of the pan. Remove from the heat and transfer to a jug or bowl. Set aside.

Bring a medium-sized saucepan of salted water to the boil. Crack the duck eggs into individual bowls and drop the eggs, separately, into the water. Reduce the heat to medium and poach the eggs for 5 minutes each, depending on size. Use a slotted spoon to remove the eggs and drain on paper towel.

To serve, spoon ⅓ cup (80 ml/2½ fl oz) of the pea soup in the middle of each serving plate. Place an egg on top, then crumble a little ricotta over each. Add the witlof leaves, then spoon the dressing over to serve.

Serves 4

4 duck eggs
100 g (3½ oz) ricotta
red-and-white witlof (chicory/Belgian endive) leaves, to serve

Pea Soup
2 tablespoons unsalted butter
½ small brown onion, diced
1–1½ cups (250–375 ml/9–13 fl oz) Chicken Stock (page 191)
140 g (5 oz) frozen peas
1 small handful of baby spinach leaves, washed (optional)
salt and freshly ground black pepper

Dressing
⅓ cup (80 ml/2½ fl oz) olive oil
100 g (3½ oz) smoked pancetta
1 clove garlic, chopped
juice of 1 lemon
100 ml (3½ fl oz) Chicken Stock (page 191)

Crayfish and Kombu Broth with Crab Tortellini

Umami is referred to as the fifth taste. As you'll see in this dish, it generates an amazing savoury flavour. Umami is found in many natural ingredients, such as tomatoes, mushrooms, parmesan cheese and kombu (Japanese seaweed), and its flavour profile is becoming just as important to the modern chef as salt and pepper.

To make the Crab Tortellini, combine the crabmeat with the egg white in a bowl. Season with salt and pepper. Spoon the mixture into a large piping bag fitted with a 2 cm (¾ inch) nozzle.

Roll a sheet of pasta out to the thinnest setting and cut into rounds using a 10 cm (4 inch) circular pastry cutter. Pipe 1 tablespoon of the crab mixture into the centre of each round. Brush around the edge of the circle with the egg, then fold the pasta over to make a semi-circle and press to seal and enclose the filling – squeeze out any air as you go. Brush the corner of the semi-circle with beaten egg. Place your index finger against the middle of the folded edge and bring the corners around your finger to meet in the middle, then press together to join. The curved edge of the pasta should flip up nicely around the filling. Remove your finger and press down gently on the filling to flatten slightly. Repeat with the remaining filling and pasta.

Put the Crayfish and Kombu Broth in a saucepan and bring to the boil. Add the tortellini and cook for 4–5 minutes, until *al dente*.

Transfer the tortellini to serving bowls and flood with the broth. Garnish with the shiso shoots and sprinkle a little cheese on top. In Italian cuisine, fish and cheese are not a match, but a little *umami-*packed Parmigiano Reggiano will enhance this dish – just don't add too much or it will overpower the delicate crab.

Serves 4–6

4 cups (1 litre/35 fl oz) Crayfish and Kombu
   Broth (page 193)
1 punnet shiso shoots
grated Parmigiano Reggiano cheese,
   to serve

Crab Tortellini
250 g (9 oz) cooked crabmeat
1 free-range egg white
salt and freshly ground black pepper
400 g (14 oz) Homemade Pasta
   (page 195)
1 free-range egg, lightly beaten

pasta

Jim~

Pasta is the ultimate comfort food in Italian cuisine. There is nothing more satisfying than a well-made pasta served with a perfectly balanced sauce. Italian pasta has had an influence on almost every cuisine and has appeared in home kitchens for decades; pasta aligns itself with almost any ingredient and that is its beauty. We are expanding on a time-honoured tradition by adding a couple of new ideas to make a point about its infinite possibilities.

This chapter is neither designed to honour, dismiss or recreate the traditional Italian pasta dishes of old. Instead of being bound by what a traditional Italian pasta should be, we encourage the creativity of the cook, using modern techniques and ingredients to explore the potential of a good Italian pasta.

Stefano ~

In this chapter we meander through homemade and commercially-available pasta varieties. We have also added a gnocchi and a couple of risottos recipes – which are not pasta at all. Forgive us for this arbitrary decision, but it was the most convenient place to park these typical Italian first courses and they are worth including and attempting at home.

Look out for the spaghetti that is cooked like a risotto (page 105). The water is gradually added with the other ingredients – once you master this method you will enjoy it immensely.

Truffle Macaroni and Cheese

A simple and fun dish. Prepare all of the ingredients first and put it together cold, then grill it in serving bowls – it makes an interesting and tasty Sunday dinner or even a midnight snack. It can also be made as a funky starter at dinner parties. We wouldn't recommend eating it every day unless you own a truffle farm. But as with almost all recipes, you can adapt it to the occasion and omit the very expensive truffle and use a good truffle paste or even a bit of truffle oil. After all, it is a play on macaroni and cheese, so it shouldn't be taken too seriously.

Serves 4

400 g (14 oz) macaroni

300 ml (10½ fl oz) Béchamel Sauce (page 187)

1 cup (100 g/3½ oz) grated Parmigiano Reggiano cheese

1 bunch chives, snipped

1 large buffalo mozzarella

1 small black truffle

Cook the macaroni in a saucepan of salted boiling water according to the packet instructions. Drain well, toss with a little oil to prevent sticking and spread out onto a clean surface to cool.

Preheat a griller (broiler) to high.

Place the macaroni in a bowl and stir in the Béchamel Sauce, half the Parmigiano Reggiano and the chives. Rip the mozzarella into small chunks and add to the macaroni. Grate half the truffle over the pasta and stir to combine.

Transfer the mixture to a baking dish or divide between four heatproof serving bowls. Sprinkle with the remaining Parmigiano Reggiano and grill (broil) until browned and the macaroni is hot. Garnish with the remaining truffle grated over the top.

Brown Butter Gnocchi with Poached Skate

This recipe will not resemble a traditional gnocchi; the dough is more like batter, a cross between gnocchi and spätzle. It is very quick to make and has none of the pain of rolling and portioning that can make gnocchi tedious to prepare. We use a piping bag and cut it with scissors straight into the pot to avoid mess. If you don't have time to make the Court Bouillon, just use salted water with a few lemons cut into it.

Serves 4–6

8 cups (2 litres/70 fl oz) Court Bouillon (page 190)
400 g (14 oz) fresh skate wing, skin removed
80 g (2¾ oz) unsalted butter
4 French shallots, finely diced
3 cloves garlic, peeled and chopped
juice of 1 lemon, plus extra lemon wedges to serve
3 tablespoons finely chopped flat-leaf (Italian) parsley
1 tablespoon capers, rinsed and drained
salt
extra-virgin olive oil, to serve

Brown Butter Gnocchi

400 g (14 oz) potatoes, such as royal blue, peeled
100 g (3½ oz) unsalted butter
1 cup (150 g/5 oz) plain (all-purpose) flour
2 x 55 g (2 oz) free-range eggs
2 tablespoons grated Parmigiano Reggiano cheese
salt

To make the Brown Butter Gnocchi, cook the potatoes in a large saucepan of salted boiling water until tender. While they are still hot, push the potatoes through a ricer or Mouli. Meanwhile, melt the butter in a small saucepan over medium heat and cook for about 4 minutes, or until the butter starts to colour. Keep cooking until it is quite dark, then add to the potato. Add the flour, eggs and cheese and mix until well combined and smooth. Set aside.

Put the Court Bouillon in a saucepan and bring to the boil, then add the skate wing. Reduce the heat so it is not a rolling boil – it does not need to be as hot as 100°C (200°F) to poach the skate. Let the skate steep in the bouillon for about 20 minutes, or until the meat is tender enough to be pulled apart with your hands.

Heat the butter in a frying pan and cook the shallot and garlic over low heat. Flake the skate into pieces, discarding the cartilage, and add to the pan, then add the lemon juice, parsley and capers, season with salt and toss to combine. Set aside and keep warm.

Spoon the gnocchi batter into a large piping bag fitted with a 2 cm (¾ inch) nozzle. Bring a large saucepan of salted water to the boil and pipe the gnocchi batter straight into the water, using kitchen scissors to cut it off into 2–4 cm (¾–1½ inch) lengths. Cook until the gnocchi floats to the surface, then remove with a slotted spoon when they are done.

Transfer the cooked gnocchi to the pan with the skate sauce. Toss and serve with lemon wedges and extra-virgin olive oil at the table.

Rigatoncini with Chicken Sauce

The sauce in this dish is fantastic when using braised home-grown chicken,
but can be equally as good using an authentic free-range chicken.
Do not smother the rigatoncini with too much sauce or even too much cheese.
The balance of sauce, pasta and cheese must be delicate.

Heat the olive oil and Lardo in a casserole large enough to fit the chicken. When the lardo has begun to melt, add the onion and celery, then add the chicken and turn to brown all over. Add the garlic, sage and rosemary to the dish, then pour in the wine and deglaze. Finally, add the tomato paste and season with salt and pepper. Cover the casserole dish with a lid, leaving the lid slightly askew so that some steam can escape. Cook for at least 1¼ hours, adding the stock gradually, about ½ cup (125 ml/4 fl oz) stock every 10 minutes or so, making sure you leave enough time between the last addition and the time when the chicken is cooked, so that the sauce is well reduced and unctuous. Shake the pan or stir from time to time.

Cook the rigatoncini in a saucepan of boiling salted water following the packet instructions. Drain well.

Remove the chicken portions and set them aside (you can eat the chicken with a salad, or shred the meat and use in sandwiches). Add the rigatoncini and the cheese to the pan with the sauce and toss to combine. If you think it needs more oomph, add a little extra butter, but take it easy, you do not want a cholesterol bomb!

Serves 4

⅓ cup (80 ml/2½ fl oz) olive oil
100 g (3½ oz) Lardo, finely chopped
    (see page 151)
1 onion, finely chopped
2 sticks celery, finely chopped
1 free-range chicken, cut into eight portions
1 clove garlic
12 sage leaves
1 sprig rosemary, finely chopped
1 cup (250 ml/9 fl oz) white wine
3 tablespoons tomato paste (concentrated
    purée)
2 cups (500 ml/17 fl oz) Chicken Stock
    (page 191)
salt and freshly ground black pepper
350 g (12 oz) rigatoncini (see note)
1 cup (100 g/3½ oz) grated Parmigiano
    Reggiano cheese

Stefano ⁓ Rigatoncini is short rigatoni. I love it. It really shows why there are different pasta shapes, hundreds of them: each suits a sauce. I like it a lot with the sauce derived from a slow-cooked chook or a duck. In our Veneto farmhouse, my mum used to place the braising pot on top of the wood-fired stove and leave it there for a long time, occasionally topping up with a little stock or hot water.

Spaghetti with Clams and Smoked Butter

Smoke and clams are a fantastic combination. If you like, you will get a similar outcome using ready-smoked clams but smoking them yourself is fun. If you can't find surf clams, pipis work well. Make more Smoked Butter than you need for this recipe and use it for other things, such as a butter sauce for salmon or spread over crostini with sardines.

Cook the pasta in a large saucepan of salted boiling water according to the packet instructions. Check the timing, because once the clams are cooked you want to get the dish to the table as quickly as possible. Drain well.

Meanwhile, heat a little olive oil in a separate saucepan over medium heat. Add the onion and garlic and cook until the onion has softened but not coloured. Increase the heat and add the clams and wine. Cover with a lid and leave the clams to steam open, about 2 minutes.

Add the Smoked Butter and tomato to the pan, shaking to incorporate, then remove the pan from the heat. Add the pasta and adjust the seasoning with salt and pepper, to taste, adding a squeeze of lemon juice, as desired. Toss through the basil, then divide the pasta and clams between serving plates, drizzle with a little extra-virgin olive oil and serve hot.

Serves 4–6

300–400 g (10½ –14 oz) spaghetti
olive oil, for cooking
1 small onion, very finely diced
2 cloves garlic, crushed
1 kg (2 lb 4 oz) fresh surf clams (or pipis)
100 ml (3½ fl oz) dry white wine
100 g (3½ oz) Smoked Butter (page 186), diced
6 fresh tomatoes, seeded and finely diced
salt and freshly ground black pepper
lemon juice, to taste
1 large handful basil, leaves torn, to serve
extra-virgin olive oil, for drizzling

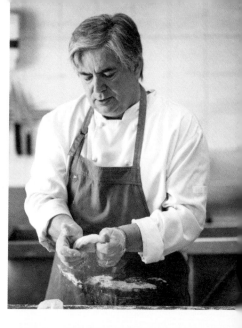

Stefano's Rabbit Papardelle with Sage and Speck

Here is a comforting, hearty pasta. The only demanding part of this recipe is dealing with the rabbits. You could also adapt this recipe to use pheasant, chicken or even duck. Whichever you use, try to also source some really good speck.

Serves 4

1 rabbit, cut into 6–8 pieces, bones left in
olive oil, for cooking
1 small carrot, finely diced
1 onion, finely diced
150 g (5½ oz) smoked speck or pancetta,
     rind removed and reserved, flesh cut into
     5 mm (¼ inch) cubes
1 large handful thyme
1 head garlic, cut in half
4 cups (1 litre/34 fl oz) Chicken Stock
     (page 191)
2 tablespoons unsalted butter
2 large handfuls sage, leaves picked
250 g (9 oz) Homemade Pasta (page 195),
     cut into about 40 thick ribbons
1 cup (100 g/3½ oz) grated Parmigiano
     Reggiano cheese
salt and freshly ground black pepper
extra-virgin olive oil, for drizzling

Preheat the oven to 160°C (315°F/Gas 2–3).

Heat a generous splash of olive oil in a large ovenproof frying pan or casserole dish over high heat. Add the rabbit pieces and cook until golden. Remove from the pan and set aside.

Add the carrot, onion, speck rind, thyme, garlic and chicken stock to the pan. Bring to the boil, return the meat to the pan, cover, then transfer to the oven and cook for 2 hours, or until the rabbit is very tender. Remove the rabbit pieces and pick off all the meat, discarding the bones. Return to the stove and reduce the liquid by half over high heat – you'll need about 2 cups (500 ml/17 fl oz), or even less.

Heat a little olive oil in a separate pan and cook the diced speck until it starts to crisp. Add the butter and sage and cook until the butter starts to brown. Add the rabbit stock and the meat.

Cook the pasta in a large saucepan of salted boiling water for about 3 minutes, or until *al dente*. Drain well and add to the sauce, then add the cheese and toss to combine. Season with salt and pepper and serve with a drizzle of extra-virgin olive oil.

Stefano ⁓ *Rabbit can stir up strong emotions in Australia. There are still people calling it 'underground mutton' in a very derisory fashion. What a pity. One of my most spectacular culinary failures was at a dinner many years ago for a well-attended wine and food society where wild rabbit was on for main course. It went down like a lead balloon. Boy, was that a wake-up call. Even now I remain very uneasy about any rabbit on a menu because I am terrified of possible bad reactions. I am not normally such a wimp, so I guess I must have been seriously traumatised that time, many years ago.*

Crayfish Ravioli with Yuzu Butter

Yuzu is a Japanese citrus fruit, which has a unique flavour and is hard to substitute. It is available in Australia in bottles from good Japanese food stores. The flavour is similar to that of grapefruit, with the acidity of a lemon. Fresh yuzu is almost impossible to find. It is usually sold salted, which is fine for this recipe, but if it is not available, use the combined juice of one lemon, one grapefruit and one lime.

Using an electric mixer, beat together the butter and yuzu until well combined. Line a baking tray with plastic wrap and spread the butter out in an even layer. Refrigerate until set.

Meanwhile, put the crayfish pieces in a bowl and season with salt and the lemon juice and toss to combine.

Roll out two sheets of the Homemade Pasta on the thinnest setting and place on a lightly floured work bench. Place the crayfish pieces onto one of the pasta sheets, evenly spaced in rows about 10 cm (4 inches) apart. Brush around each piece of crayfish with a little beaten egg. Lay the other pasta sheet on top and use your fingers to press down to seal the pasta sheet around the meat and remove any air bubbles. Use an 8–10 cm (3¼–4 inch) fluted round pastry cutter to cut out individual ravioli and arrange them on a baking tray dusted with semolina.

Cook the ravioli in a large saucepan of salted boiling water for 4–5 minutes or until *al dente*. Drain well.

Meanwhile, melt the yuzu butter in a large saucepan over medium heat. Add the capers and the stock. Bring to the boil briefly and add the pasta. Add the mascarpone – this will help bring the sauce together. Remove from the heat. Toss the pasta in the pan to combine all the ingredients. Add the fennel and parsley and season with salt and pepper, to taste. Serve immediately.

Serves 4

100 g (3½ oz) cultured unsalted butter, softened at room temperature
2½ tablespoons (50 ml/1¾ fl oz) yuzu juice
½ raw crayfish tail, shell removed and flesh chopped into 2 cm (¾ inch) pieces
salt
juice of ½ lemon
¼ quantity Homemade Pasta (page 194)
1 free-range egg, lightly beaten
semolina, for dusting
1 tablespoon capers, rinsed and drained
½ cup Crayfish and Kombu Broth (page 193), Chicken Stock (page 191) or Fish Stock (page 193)
1 tablespoon mascarpone
1 teaspoon chopped wild fennel, dill or basil
1 teaspoon chopped flat-leaf (Italian) parsley
salt and freshly ground black pepper

Bolognese

Stefano ⁓ A traditional Bolognese employs only a little tomato paste and no herbs or garlic as is typical in many English-speaking countries. As there are many versions of Bolognese sauce I went to the *Accademia Italiana Della Cucina*, the Italian Academy of Cooking, to check out their official recipe. It confirmed what I knew but they added a little milk during the cooking process and used pancetta, whereas I use minced pork shoulder in my recipe (page 100). You can add some duck liver or minced veal or porcini mushrooms if you wish to have a more complex sauce.

Jim ～ I am born-and-bred Australian so I guess most Italians would argue that I don't understand a good Bolognese. I have cooked, eaten and experienced the beauty of this simple dish more times than I can count; though I wasn't raised on it in my youth, I have made up for it in my later years. My version (page 101) is not simple and fast. If you want to produce a beautiful – and quick – Bolognese, Stefano's is the best I have tasted, but give both a try and decide for yourself. Wagyu tail can be hard to get, in which case oxtail, osso bucco or a good brisket can be used in its place.

Stefano's Classic Bolognese Sauce

Serves 4

2 tablespoons (40 g/1½ oz) unsalted
    butter
⅓ cup (80 ml/2½ fl oz) olive oil
1 small onion, diced
1 stick celery, diced
1 carrot, diced
200 g (7 oz) coarsely minced
    (ground) beef skirt
200 g (7 oz) minced (ground) pork
    shoulder
½ cup (125 ml/4 fl oz) red wine
80 g (2¾ oz) tomato paste
    (concentrated purée)
1 cup (250 ml/9 fl oz) full-cream
    (whole) milk
salt and freshly ground black pepper

Heat the butter with the olive oil in a large saucepan over medium heat heat. Add the onion, celery and carrot and cook until the onion has softened but not coloured. Add the beef and pork mince and stir until it has coloured. Add the wine and tomato paste and cook gently, adding milk from time to time and seasoning with salt and pepper. Cook for about 2–3 hours, adding a bit of water to keep things moist, if needed. Any longer and the meat loses its fragrance, in my opinion.

The above quantity is enough to serve four people with pasta – in Italy they prefer to serve bolognese with fettuccine or similar homemade pasta.

Jim's Spaghetti Bolognese

Serves 4

1 kg (2 lb 4 oz) roma (plum)
    tomatoes, whole
300 g (10½ oz) Homemade Pasta
    (page 195), cut into spaghetti
1 cup (100 g/3½ oz) grated
    Parmigianino Reggiano cheese,
    plus extra for garnish
extra-virgin olive oil, for drizzling
4 Parmesan Crisps (page 185)
1 punnet basil shoots

Wagyu Tail

1 wagyu tail, cut into sections along
    its joints
salt and freshly ground black pepper
½ cup (250 ml/9 fl oz) olive oil
1 carrot, diced
1 stick celery, diced
1 onion, diced
6 cloves garlic, whole
1 tablespoon tomato paste
    (concentrated purée)
3 cups (750 ml/25 fl oz) dry red wine
8 cups (2 litres/34 fl oz) Beef Stock
    (page 192)
2 sprigs rosemary
3 bay leaves

To prepare the Wagyu Tail, preheat the oven to 160°C. Season the meat with salt and pepper. Heat the oil in a large ovenproof pot or casserole and brown the meat in batches. Set the meat aside, pour off some of the oil and add the vegetables and garlic. Cook until lightly coloured. Add the tomato paste and cook for a further 5 minutes on low heat. Add half the red wine, and simmer until the vegetables begin to fry again. Add the rest of the red wine and reduce again. Add the Beef Stock, rosemary and bay leaves and bring to the boil. Return the meat to the sauce and cook in the oven for about 6 hours, or until the meat is falling off the bone. Remove the meat from the sauce and set aside to cool. Shred the meat and set aside until needed. Meanwhile, Strain the sauce through a sieve and, using a ladle, push as much of the vegetables through the strainer as you can. Allow the sauce to cool for 10–15 minutes until the fat rises to the top. Skim and discard the fat. Stir about 200 ml (7 fl oz) of the sauce through the meat. Set the remaining sauce aside until needed.

Preheat the oven to 180°C (350°F/Gas 4). Place the tomatoes on a tray and roast for 15–20 minutes until they are soft. Allow to cool then peel. Blend the tomatoes until smooth. Pass through a sieve, using a ladle to push through. Discard the pulp.

Combine the tomato purée and remaining wagyo tail sauce (without the meat) in a large pot and reduce over high heat by about two-thirds. You should end up with an amazingly rich red sauce that holds its shape when spooned onto a plate. Check for seasoning and adjust if necessary.

In a large saucepan, warm the wagyu tail meat over low heat. Cook the spaghetti for about 2 minutes in plenty of salted boiling water, drain, and add to the meat. Add the cheese and drizzle with extra-virgin olive oil.

To serve, twirl the pasta around a carving fork to form a cylinder of meaty pasta you can stand up. Place dots of the tomato reduction on the plate and top the pasta with a Parmesan Crisp. Garnish with some more olive oil, and a sprinkle of cheese and basil shoots.

Pearl Barley Risotto

Here is a risotto for the vegetarians. Pearl barley is very tough, so it takes a while to cook as a risotto, but patience will reward, and if you like a bit of *al dente* food, this is for you. We prefer real spinach, not the loose leaves. If using real spinach, wash it at least three times. Blanch in a pot of hot, salted water for a few seconds, cool and squeeze dry. Chop and add to the risotto towards the end.

Serves 4

olive oil, for cooking
1 large brown onion, chopped
2 cloves garlic, chopped
1 red capsicum (pepper), seeded
    and chopped
1 yellow capsicum (pepper), seeded
    and chopped
4 fresh tomatoes, peeled and chopped
1 potato, thinly sliced
200 g (7 oz) pearl barley
1 bay leaf
12 cups (3 litres/105 fl oz) Vegetable Stock
    (page 191) or Chicken Stock (page 191),
    simmering
several handfuls English spinach leaves,
    blanched in boiling water then drained
    and chopped
1 cup (100 g/3½ oz) grated Parmigiano
    Reggiano cheese
60 g (2 oz) soft goat's cheese
1 tablespoon chopped preserved lemon
    (optional)

Heat a little olive oil in a large saucepan over medium–high heat. Add the onion, garlic and capsicum and cook until soft and tender. Add the tomato and cook for a little longer, then add the potato and cook for 3 minutes more.

Add the barley and bay leaf to the pan, and then add the stock, a little at a time, stirring constantly – barley will not absorb stock like rice, so go slowly and continue stirring and do not panic. You can leave this alone (unlike rice). It is more a case of cooking the barley and allowing the stock to evaporate. There's no harm if your risotto is a little runny – you can change its name and call it *minestra* (soup). Add the spinach, stir in the Parmigiano Reggiano and goat's cheese and toss in the preserved lemon, if using.

Stefano's Risotto with Durello

Durello is a dry sparkling wine from the hills of Verona. You can use a dry prosecco, or indeed any dry sparkling wine. I mention durello because of my interest in alternative varieties and also to be true to a great classic from the Verona region, where a terrific semi-hard cheese called Monte Veronese also comes from and completes the risotto. Seek it out from importers or replace with other semi-hard cheeses like Piave or Montasio, which are more readily available.

Serves 4

olive oil, for cooking
100 g (3½ oz) unsalted butter
1 onion, finely chopped
250 g (9 oz) Italian risotto rice
200 ml (7 fl oz) durello or other dry sparkling
  wine, such as prosecco
8 cups (2 litres/70 fl oz) Chicken Stock
  (page 191)
1 cup (100 g/3½ oz) grated Parmigiano
  Reggiano cheese
salt
1 cup (100 g/3½ oz) grated semi-hard
  cheese such as Monte Veronese,
  Piave or Montasio

Heat a little olive oil with half of the butter in a large saucepan over high heat. Add the onion and cook until translucent but not coloured. Add the rice and stir for a minute or so, until the rice is well coated. When the rice begins to stick to the base of the pan, add some wine, allow to evaporate and then add a generous amount of stock, initially flooding the rice and stirring constantly. Continue to stir and add the stock and wine alternately as it is absorbed by the rice. Season with salt, if needed. You may not need to use all the stock; the rice should not be too wet or too soft.

Place the pan on an even work surface and drop in the remaining butter and the cheeses. It may seem like a lot, but this is where the umami flavour is found! Using the handle of the pan or both handles, push the pan forward with a vigorous movement, so that the rice rises in an upward wave. As you get more and more confident this will become easier. The higher you push the rice, the greater the aeration and the more creamy and integrated the rice will be. I have seen some Venetian chefs pushing the wave as high as 40–50 cm (16–20 inches) from the base of the pot. It looks difficult and acrobatic, so go slow initially or you'll end up with hot rice all over your kitchen – a dozen flicks or so will be enough. If you are not too confident, just stir with a wooden spoon. Serve at once.

Spaghetti Cooked in Its Sauce

Stefano ∼ Accompany this dish with a delicious pilsener. I like the idea of a spicy dish with the lingering bitterness of a refreshing beer. The method here is unconventional but gives a great result.

Heat the butter with a little olive oil in a frying pan over medium–high heat and add the sausage and fry until nicely coloured and cooked through. Set aside.

Heat some olive oil in a large frying pan over medium heat. Add the garlic and chilli and cook until coloured. Add the cherry tomatoes and cook for 1 minute. Season with salt and pepper.

Heat a saucepan of boiling salted water. Add the spaghetti to the frying pan and sprinkle it over the tomatoes. Add two small ladlefuls of the hot water (this floods the pan a bit like when cooking risotto). Bring to a simmer and shake the pan or separate the spaghetti with a wooden spoon. When the liquid has reduced, add more water; eventually the spaghetti will lose its stiffness. Continue in this manner and taste as you go (when you are more familiar with the process you will be able to easily gauge how things are developing).

When the pasta is nearly cooked add the sausage and the basil and other herbs as desired.

Continue cooking until the liquid has reduced. Should the spaghetti feel nearly cooked and you think you have too much liquid in the pan then simply pour it out – but this should be avoided if possible.

Sprinkle generously with the cheese and drizzle with extra-virgin olive oil if you like the flavour and serve.

Serves 2

1 teaspoon unsalted butter

olive oil, for cooking

1 large pork sausage, skin removed and
    broken into small pieces or use
      100 g (3½ oz) coarsely minced (ground)
      pork that has been well seasoned

2 cloves garlic, chopped

1 red chilli, seeded and finely chopped

1 punnet cherry tomatoes, chopped

salt and freshly ground black pepper

100 g (3½ oz) spaghetti

1 handful basil leaves

1 handful of chopped herbs such as parsley
    or chives (optional)

1 handful freshly grated Parmigiano
    Reggiano cheese

extra-virgin olive oil, for drizzling (optional)

fish & seafood

Jim~

The Mildura region is abundant with freshwater aquaculture. One of my fondest memories growing up on the Murray River as a kid was hauling up nets full of large blue-claw yabbies and cooking them over a fire in a large homemade pot laden with rock salt. My father used to hang the pot from a tree to cool when they were done. To this day I can still remember the excitement and the anticipation that aroma used to bring. Wild and farmed freshwater yabbies are among the best eating crustaceans in the country.

Seafood is such a versatile and compatible protein. Recent trends in *sous vide* cooking have inspired a whole new way of preparing seafood, rescuing it from the deep-fryer or the harsh heat of the pan. Most seafood can be 'cooked' at a much lower temperature than red meat.

A good tip for testing when white fish is cooked properly is to push a toothpick into the flesh: if there is a lot of resistance it is raw. It should slide in but feel firm. For oily or red fish, personal choice is paramount, so experiment. An exception to this rule is white fish such as kingfish or swordfish, which can be eaten rare.

Spaghetti Cooked in Its Sauce

Stefano ⁓ Accompany this dish with a delicious pilsener. I like the idea of a spicy dish with the lingering bitterness of a refreshing beer. The method here is unconventional but gives a great result.

Heat the butter with a little olive oil in a frying pan over medium–high heat and add the sausage and fry until nicely coloured and cooked throughout. Set aside.

Heat some olive oil in large frying pan over medium heat. Add the garlic and chilli and cook until coloured. Add the cherry tomatoes and cook for 1 minute. Season with salt and pepper.

Heat a saucepan of lightly salted water. Add the spaghetti to the frying pan and spread it out over the tomatoes. Add two small ladlefuls of the hot water (this floods the pan a bit like when cooking risotto). Bring to a simmer and shake the pan or separate the spaghetti with a wooden spoon. When the liquid has reduced, add more water; eventually the spaghetti will lose its stiffness. Continue in this manner and taste as you go (when you are more familiar with the process you will be able to easily gauge how things are developing).

When the pasta is nearly cooked, add the sausage and the basil and other herbs as desired.

Continue cooking until the liquid has reduced. Should the spaghetti feel nearly cooked and you think you have too much liquid in the pan then simply pour it out – but that should be avoided if possible.

Sprinkle generously with the cheese and drizzle with extra-virgin olive oil if you like the flavour and gloss.

Serves 2

1 teaspoon unsalted butter

olive oil, for cooking

1 large pork sausage, skin removed and broken into small pieces or use 100 g (3½ oz) coarsely minced (ground) pork that has been well seasoned

2 cloves garlic, chopped

1 red chilli, seeded and finely chopped

1 punnet cherry tomatoes, chopped

salt and freshly ground black pepper

100 g (3½ oz) spaghetti

1 handful basil leaves

1 handful of chopped herbs such as parsley or chives (optional)

1 handful freshly grated Parmigiano Reggiano cheese

extra-virgin olive oil, for drizzling (optional)

Stefano~

The fame and success of Stefano's restaurant was initially established by the daily use of Murray River bounty. One critic, Stephen Downes of the *Herald Sun*, was so impressed by a meal of yabbies and cod, he gave us a score of 19 out of 20! When the ban on river fish was introduced I felt like closing the restaurant. The ban continues because illegal fishing is persisting and it was not accompanied by a reduction in recreational fishing, which is overall much more harmful – but that is another story.

Luckily, some large aquaculture investments have been successful and farmed fish can be purchased. In the restaurant I have kept things simple, but it is fun watching Jim doing crazy things with seafood, such as serving sweet macadamias next to yabbies or prawns or serving trevalla with prosecco sauce.

Rolled King George Whiting Stuffed with Prawns

This is a really simple and fun recipe with a little bit of class that is not going to take you hours to prepare: it can literally be cooked in twenty minutes. The sauce can be omitted and the seafood baked in the oven with a bit of olive oil and a squeeze of lemon.

Preheat the oven to 190°C (375°F/gas 5).

Heat a little olive oil in a frying pan over high heat. When the pan is very hot, add the prawns and fry briefly to gain a bit of colour but don't cook through, about 10 seconds will do. Remove from the pan and set aside in a bowl.

Add the onions and garlic to the pan and cook until the onion has softened, then remove and add to the bowl with the prawns. Transfer to a food processor and process until to make a very coarse puree. Add the egg and breadcrumbs and pulse again until the mixture comes together. Add the lemon juice, then transfer to a bowl and refrigerate until needed.

Remove the small pin-bones from the whiting with fish pliers. Place the fillets, skin side down, on a clean work surface and season with salt.

Spread the prawn mixture evenly along the flesh-side of the fillet. Starting from the thick end, roll it toward tail so you get a nice cylinder. Secure the roll with a skewer or toothpick and place upright on a tray. Repeat with each fillet.

Place the Napoli Sauce in a mixing bowl with the olives, cherry tomatoes, basil and capers. Season with salt, pepper and the sugar. Spoon the sauce around the whiting and bake in the oven for 10 minutes. The fish and sauce can be served with a green salad.

Serves 4

olive oil, for cooking

300 g (10½ oz) raw prawns (shrimp), peeled and deveined

½ red onion, diced

3 cloves garlic, thinly sliced

1 free-range egg

1 cup (80 g/3 oz) fresh breadcrumbs

juice of 1 lemon

4 large whiting fillets, skin and tail left on

salt

1 cup (250 ml/8½ fl oz) Napoli Sauce (page 194)

½ cup (100 g/3½ oz) baby green olives, pitted

1 punnet cherry tomatoes

1 handful ripped basil leaves

1 tablespoon capers, rinsed and drained

freshly ground black pepper

a pinch of caster (superfine) sugar

Poached Baby Snapper Fillets with Ricotta, Scallop and Macadamia

This recipe features our take on a classic fish velouté. Veloutés have sadly gone out of fashion; they have been replaced by foams and airs. This recipe is made with olive oil instead of flour and butter and is quite different. Give it a go, it is a perfect base for a soup as well.

Serves 4

150 g (5½ oz) scallops, roe removed, cleaned

salt

2 egg whites

50 g (1¾ oz) crushed macadamia nuts

50 g (1¾ oz) ricotta

50 ml (1¾ fl oz) pouring (whipping) cream

1 tablespoon chopped flat-leaf (Italian) parsley

8 × 80–100 g (3–3½ oz) boneless baby snapper fillets

2 cups (500 ml/17 fl oz) Fish and Olive Oil Velouté (page 189), heated

baby shoots, to garnish

Chill the bowl of a food processor in the freezer so it is very cold (you don't want the scallop meat to get warm at all or the mix will split and be grainy). Place the scallops and a pinch of salt into the food processor and process on high speed until smooth. Scrape down the sides of the bowl a few times to make sure it is evenly combined. Add the egg whites and blend to incorporate. Transfer to a mixing bowl and stir through the macadamias, ricotta and cream. Add the parsley and season with salt.

Wipe down a clean work surface with a damp cloth and place a layer of plastic wrap on top, about 50 cm (20 inches) long. Place another layer on top of the first.

Put one snapper fillet, skin side down, on the plastic wrap and spread 2–3 tablespoons of the scallop and ricotta mixture evenly along the fillet. Place another fillet on top of this and roll into a cylinder. Tie each end of the plastic wrap, ensuring the barrel of fish is tight. Repeat with some more plastic wrap and the remaining fillets to make four fish parcels. (It will take some practice to get these into a nice-looking cylinder shape – don't stress too much about how it looks, it will taste delicious regardless.)

Bring a large saucepan of water to the boil. Lower the fish parcels into the water, then turn off the heat Allow the fish to sit in the liquid and poach for about 20 minutes.

To serve, slice one end of the plastic wrap and remove the fish. Serve on the Fish and Olive Oil Velouté, garnished with baby shoots.

Baked Trevalla with Prosecco Sauce

Prosecco and Champagne both will make a great sauce for most fish and seafood.
They have great flavours and, mixed with a little butter or cream,
make for a very quick and satisfying sauce. Always add a little more prosecco
at the end of making the sauce to add some freshness and spritz.

Preheat the oven to 180°C (350°F/Gas 4).

Heat a little olive oil in a large ovenproof frying pan. When the oil is smoking hot, season the fish with salt and place it in the pan, skin-side down. Remove from the heat immediately, transfer to the oven and cook for 5–8 minutes, or until a toothpick slides into the flesh with little resistance – as the fish rests it will finish cooking. Remove the fish from the pan and set aside; discard the oil from the pan.

Return the pan to high heat and deglaze the pan with three-quarters of the prosecco. Add the stock, thyme and garlic and cook on high heat until the liquid has reduced to about ½ cup (125 ml/4 fl oz).

Remove the pan from the heat and add the butter, swirling the pan to incorporate. Add the remaining prosecco to give the sauce some freshness. Add the cream, parsley and lemon juice, season with salt and keep warm (not too hot, or the sauce will separate) until ready to serve.

Place the fish on serving plates with some steamed greens or a salad of your choice and spoon over the prosecco sauce.

Serves 4

4 × 150 g (5½ oz) blue-eye trevalla fillets,
    deboned
olive oil, for cooking
salt
1 cup (250 ml/9 fl oz) prosecco
½ cup (125 ml/4 fl oz) Fish Stock
    (page 193) or Chicken Stock (page 191)
2 sprigs thyme
1 clove garlic
2 tablespoons unsalted butter, diced
50 ml (1¾ fl oz) pouring (whipping) cream
1 tablespoon chopped flat-leaf (Italian)
    parsley
juice of 1 lemon

Tommy Ruff Baked in Hay

This method of cooking imparts a great smoky flavour to the fish.
The cooking needs to be done on a barbecue chargrill, or even in the coals of a fire,
as the hay needs to burn a little.

Serves 4 as a starter

2 small handfuls hay
8 whole small tommy ruff or large sardines,
    cleaned and gutted (ask your fishmonger
    to do this for you)
16–20 slices pancetta
salt
lemon wedges, to serve

Herb Stuffing
olive oil, for cooking
1 onion, diced
2 cloves garlic, crushed
300 g (10½ oz) fresh breadcrumbs
1 tablespoon chopped flat-leaf (Italian)
    parsley
1 tablespoon chopped basil
1 tablespoon chopped sage
finely grated zest of 1 lemon
juice of 1 lemon

Preheat a barbecue grill to high.

To make the Herb Stuffing, heat a little olive oil in a frying pan over medium heat. Add the onion and garlic and cook until the onion has softened. Transfer to a large bowl and add the breadcrumbs, parsely, basil and sage. Season, and moisten with a little more oil if needed. Add the lemon juice and zest and set aside.

Cut out eight large squares of foil that will be large enough to wrap the fish and some hay. Make a bed of hay in the centre of each piece of foil.

Pack the stuffing into the cavity of each fish, then wrap each one in pancetta. Place the fish on top of the hay, season with salt and wrap the foil tightly around each fish to enclose.

Place the foil parcels on the hot grill and cook for 5–8 minutes on each side.

Place each parcel on a plate for diners to unwrap at the table. Serve with lemon wedges alongside.

Carpaccio

Stefano ～ The size of fish you choose for this recipe (page 118) will determine the quantity of ingredients you will need. Four tablespoons of each of the seeds and one tablespoon of salt is a good start, but if you have extra seasoning, you can use it on something else, like roast pork. I do not like much else on my carpaccio other than a little good-quality oil and a little salt. Any other flavour obscures the delicate tuna taste.

Jim ～ Tuna carpaccio is one of those dishes that has stayed in the restaurant, no matter how many chefs pass through. I have not departed from the comfort of the old faithful but I have modernised it (page 119). The addition of popcorn originally came from a beer-matching dinner Stefano and I did; I created this dish to go with the award-winning Sun Light Mildura Brewery Beer and served the pocorn in little paper cups with the tuna carpaccio in the centre of the table. It was a hit; not only did the popcorn work with the beer but it was a perfect accompaniment to the tuna. Any style of salted popcorn is fine.

Stefano's Carpaccio of Tuna

Serves 4

4 tablespoons coriander seeds
4 tablespoons fennel seeds
salt flakes
extra-virgin olive oil, for cooking,
    plus extra to serve
1 large fillet (around 500g/1 lb 2 oz)
    of the best tuna available
2 tablespoons olive oil
1 tablespoon washed baby capers
½ cucumber, peeled deseeded and
    finely diced
watercress shoots, to garnish
grissini or light homemade bread,
    to serve

Grind the coriander and fennel seeds with a little salt using a mortar and pestle, to form a powder. Transfer the ground spices to a tray.

Lightly brush a little extra-virgin olive oil over the fish and roll in the spices to coat evenly.

Heat the olive oil in a non-stick frying pan over medium–high heat and lightly seal the fish on all sides. Remove from the heat, allow to cool slightly then wrap the fish tightly in plastic wrap until ready to serve. Using a sharp knife, slice the fish thinly and place directly onto serving plates.

Top with a little extra-virgin olive oil, a sprinkling of salt flakes, capers, cucumber and watercress, and serve with grissini or bread.

Jim's Tuna Carpaccio with Sesame Seeds and Salted Popcorn

Serves 4–6

½ cup salted popped popcorn

300 g (10½ oz) sashimi-grade
    yellowfin tuna fillet

plain (all-purpose) flour, for dusting

2 cups (300 g/10½ oz) sesame
    seeds

3 free-range egg whites, lightly
    whisked

100 ml (3½ fl oz) extra-virgin olive oil

1 tablespoon snipped chives (with
    flowers if you can get them)

Use a spice grinder or food processor to grind half of the popcorn to a coarse powder.

Cut the tuna into 10 cm × 5 cm (8 inch × 2 inch) pieces (as close to rectangular as you can get) following the length of the grain. Dust the tuna in the flour to coat evenly, patting off any excess with your hand.

Place the sesame seeds in wide shallow dish. Toss the tuna in the egg whites to cover, then roll in the sesame seeds to coat.

Heat 2 tablespoons of the oil in a large frying pan. Add the tuna and sear on each side for about 10 seconds, or until the sesame seeds are lightly browned – remember this is a carpaccio, so you don't want to cook the tuna.

Remove the tuna from the pan and cut into 5 mm (¼ inch) slices. Arrange the slices on plates and drizzle with the remaining olive oil. Scatter the popcorn, popcorn powder and chives over the top.

Cured Rainbow Trout with Citrus Horseradish and Wild Fennel

When cured, rainbow trout has an amazing sweet flavour that is hard to beat. This dish uses the same curing method as the Smoked Salmon (page 154) but is cured for less time because the fish are smaller. In our opinion, rainbow trout taste better than their sea-dwelling counterparts when cured.

Serves 4

1 kg Basic Cure (page 184)
4 × 150 g (5½ oz) skinless, boneless rainbow trout fillets
4 tablespoons chopped fennel tips
2 tablespoons chopped wild fennel
2 teaspoons chopped French shallots
1 grapefruit
1 blood orange
2 tablespoons capers, rinsed, drained and chopped
100 ml (3½ fl oz) extra-virgin olive oil
juice of 1 lemon
freshly grated horseradish, to serve

Place half the Basic Cure mixture in a tray of similar size to the fish. Place the fish, skin side down, on the cure. Cover with the remaining cure mixture. The fish must be buried in the mixture for effective results. Wrap with plastic wrap and place in the refrigerator for 5 hours. Remove after 5 hours and wash off the cure.

Place the fish in the freezer, not to freeze, but to get them as cold as possible to make them easier to slice – you need to slice the fish as thinly as possible.

Combine the fennel, wild fennel and shallots in a bowl and mix well.

Peel and segment the grapefruit and blood orange, removing any white pith and seeds.

Arrange the fish on serving plates. Sprinkle the herb mix liberally over the sliced fish. Do the same with the capers and follow with the citrus. Garnish with lots of olive oil, a squeeze of lemon juice and some freshly grated horseradish, to taste.

Stefano ⁓ *Wild fennel is widely available along southern Australian dirt road-sides and river banks. Use dill if not available.*

Yabby Tails with Saffron Sauce, Braised Chicory and Fregola

Although saffron is a perfect partner for most seafood, it is especially good with yabbies and cod; the earthy flavour of saffron works in perfect harmony with the fish's earthy river taste. You can replace the yabbies with prawns (shrimp) or other seafood, but freshwater fish works better.

To make the Saffron Sauce, combine the wine, vinegar, lemon juice and saffron in a saucepan over high heat. Boil over high heat until the liquid has reduced by half. Add the stock and bring back to the boil, then reduce by half again. Pour into a suitable bowl or jug, then, using a hand-held stick blender or whisk, blend in the butter one piece at a time until well combined. Keep warm.

Bring a saucepan of salted water to the boil and blanch the chicory for about 2 minutes, or until just tender. Drain well.

Add the yabby tails, fregola and chicory to the saffron sauce and stir over low heat to combine and heat through. Season with salt and lemon juice and serve in large bowls. Garnish with the tomato and spring onion.

Serves 4 as a starter

10 chicory (witlof) stems, cut into 5 cm (2 inch) batons
24 cooked yabby (freshwater crayfish) tails (refer to cooking instructions on page 58 if you prefer to buy the yabbies raw)
150 g (5½ oz) cooked fregola or Israeli couscous
salt
lemon juice, to taste
2 tomatoes, peeled, seeded and diced
2 spring onions (scallions), green part only, finely chopped

Saffron Sauce

300 ml (10½ fl oz) white wine
2 tablespoons white wine vinegar
juice of 1 lemon
a large pinch of saffron threads
300 ml (10½ fl oz) Chicken Stock (page 191)
150 g (5 oz) unsalted butter, cut into cubes

the whole beast, offal & game

Jim ~

Given today's fast-paced lifestyle, coupled with modern supermarket convenience, the art of preparing and using all parts of a whole animal is becoming increasingly redundant. The ease of pre-portioned, pre-diced and pre-sliced meat cannot be denied, even though it has led to excessive amounts of over-processed food becoming the food of choice.

Most of us have no idea where our food comes from or what is in it. Modern society is increasingly losing its connection with nature and the simple pleasures of preparing ingredients and cooking them using simple age-old techniques – this is something past generations would have taken for granted.

There is something primal about preparing a whole lamb or a wild hare that is hard to explain. This chapter captures the joy of preparing whole animals and will provide you with the skills to do so yourself.

Stefano～

What Jim says is all true and well said. However, people are not to be blamed for losing touch with each part of the animal. Supermarkets have done the damage in Australia, sorry to say. As I am writing this I am thinking of the small supermarket in my Italian village, Dosson, near Treviso.

The meat refrigerator is arranged like this, from left to right: young calf liver, older liver, segmented veal hearts, lung pieces, pork trotters, tripe (cooked and raw), horse mince, pork hocks, tendons, cotechino, sausages, all boiling meats, pork, veal, beef (all cuts), turkey, rabbit, rabbit back legs, ducks, duck fillets, quail, guinea fowl, chicken, all chicken parts (boilers, half-boilers, livers, giblets), and so on.

People will consume each part of the animal *if* it is offered to them. And if the choice is there, a gastronomy obviously follows.

As I am writing I am also thinking of a recent trip to Palermo where the street vendors serve soft bread rolls topped with sesame seeds and filled with sliced spleen and lung cooked in massive amounts of pork fat. The bun comes plain and saturated with the lard or with the addition of ricotta and a squirt of lemon. How divine!

Boneless Side of Lamb Stuffed with Braised Leg, Wrapped in Crepinette

Crepinette is the caul fat that holds the stomach in place. It is a lacy webbing and is great for wrapping meats for roasting or poaching since it goes translucent and is hardly detectable after cooking but helps retain moisture. This recipe shows you how to use a whole side of lamb. The fatty shoulder and leg give moisture to the loin, so it can be cooked for a while longer before it dries out. The lamb should reach medium and no more.

Serves 8–10

1 side of lamb, no larger than 6 kg
(13 lb 8 oz)
olive oil, for cooking
2 onions, chopped
3 carrots, peeled and diced
3 sticks celery, diced
2 tablespoons tomato paste (concentrated purée)
3 cups (750 ml/25 fl oz) red wine
1 head garlic, cut in half
1 large handful rosemary, reserving a few sprigs for garnish
4 sprigs thyme
salt and freshly ground black pepper
4 litres (140 fl oz) Dark Lamb Stock
(page 192) or Beef Stock (page 192)
300 g (10½ oz) crepinette

Remove the leg and shoulder from the side of lamb. Cut down the spine following the loin and carefully separate the loin from the bone. Run a knife down the rib cage, removing the belly and the loin in one piece. Trim the skin and some of the fat from the belly and trim the edges so it is a nice even rectangle. Refrigerate until ready to use.

Preheat the oven to 140°C (275°F/Gas 1).

Heat a little olive oil in a large casserole dish and add the onion, carrot and celery. Cook until the vegetables are coloured, then add the tomato paste and cook for a further 10 minutes. Add the wine, garlic, rosemary and thyme and cook until most of the wine has evaporated. Add the stock and bring to the boil, then add the lamb leg and shoulder, cover, and braise in the oven for about 4 hours.

Remove the meat from the dish and when cool enough to handle, pick the meat from the bones, discarding the bones. Season the meat with salt and pepper and some of the extra rosemary. Allow to cool.

Skim the cooking liquid in the dish and strain into a clean saucepan, using a ladle to push through as much of the cooked vegetables as possible. Reduce over high heat to a coating consistency. Set aside – this will be used to sauce the finished lamb.

Increase the oven temperature to 180°C (350°F/Gas 4).

Take the lamb loin and belly out of the refrigerator. Spread out the crepinette in one layer on a work surface and place the lamb loin and belly on top, flesh side up. Season with salt and pepper, and place about the braised meat in the centre. Roll the loin over the braised meat into a cylinder and wrap with the crepinette. Fold the edges of the crepinette under the meat and roast in the oven for 30–45 minutes, or until the meat is cooked to medium. Rest for at least 15 minutes before serving. Serve the lamb sliced with fresh vegetables or a simple salad and the sauce.

Lamb or Goat in One Tray

Unlike precise modern cooking, the quantities in this recipe are purely indicative, which is the beauty of this dish. It is about intuition, not precision.

Serves 6 or more

2 kg (4 lb 8 oz) lamb or young goat
   shoulder, cut into chunky pieces
10 cloves garlic, left whole and unpeeled
10 tomatoes, skinned, seeded and chopped
1 small handful of sage
extra-virgin olive oil, for cooking
salt and freshly ground black pepper
1 cup (100 g/3½ oz) grated pecorino cheese
a generous sprinkling of fresh breadcrumbs
1 glass dry white wine

Preheat the oven to 170°C (325°F/Gas 3). Line a roasting tin large enough to hold all the meat with baking paper.

Arrange the meat on the tray and scatter over the garlic, tomato and sage. Pour in the wine, 2 glasses of water and drizzle a good slurping of olive oil over the meat. Season generously with salt and pepper and sprinkle the pecorino and breadcrumbs on top. Cover the tray with baking paper, then with foil.

Place the tray in the oven and let it cook undisturbed for at least 2 hours before checking. Depending on the quality or age of the meat, it may take between 3–4 hours to finish cooking. Remove the foil and paper during the last 20 minutes of cooking (or it may take longer) to get a nice golden crust on top.

Serve with roasted potatoes, and greens. I like bitter greens cooked in more garlic and a little dried chilli.

Stefano ᠆ This is simple food from yesteryear, when nothing was wasted and protein was precious, whether it came from the neck or the butt. Meat on the bone was mixed irrespective of where it came from and you cooked it slowly until tender. Cooking times can vary a lot, depending on the age and quality of the animal. I prefer younger carcasses for this purpose, especially if dealing with goat. Tender spring lamb is also delicious. You can purchase the shoulder for this dish if you do not care for the entire animal. You would need a big party for that.

Stefano's Farmed Rabbit Old-Style

This is a recipe from my sister-in-law Milena, who farms her own rabbits and gets my brother Tony to prepare them. He tells me he finds the killing process repugnant and always closes his eyes when doing it. He also bans everyone from the shed and talks sweetly to the rabbits before the final act. Make the sauce the day before for best results.

To make the Sauce, heat the olive oil and butter in a large saucepan. Add the onion and garlic and cook until the onion has softened. Add the beef and pork and cook over medium heat. Add enough hot water to cover and keep things moist for at least 1 hour. Reduce the heat to low, then add the liver, anchovies and capers and cook for a further 1 hour, adding extra water to keep things moist. When the meat is soft, like a Bolognese, add the pepper. The sauce should be peppery, of a nice consistency, slightly salty and piquant. Remove from the heat, allow to cool and refrigerate overnight for the flavours to develop.

Preheat the oven to 180°C (350°F/Gas 4). Line a roasting tin with baking paper.

Heat a little olive oil in a large saucepan over medium heat. Add the onion and cook until it has softened, then remove from the heat and add to a large bowl with the combined pork, beef and chicken, the breadcrumbs, parsley, sage, egg and cheese, and season with salt and pepper. If you like, cook a little sample to taste and adjust the seasoning accordingly. Place the rabbit on to a clean bench, spread the stuffing over the rabbit, roll, then truss with kitchen string.

Drizzle a little extra olive oil over the rabbit, rubbing it in and season. Roast in the oven for up to 45 minutes, or until golden. Remove from the oven and rest for 15 minutes in a warm place.

To serve, reheat the sauce. Slice the rabbit and place on warmed serving plates. Baste with the cooking juices. Serve the sauce in a jug or gravy boat alongside. Accompany the roast with hot slices of grilled polenta (page 15). Any leftover sauce is good for crostini or more grilled polenta. It will keep well refrigerated in an airtight container for up to 5 days.

Serves 4–5

1 large farmed rabbit, up to 2 kg (4 lb 8 oz), deboned (ask your butcher to do this)
olive oil, for cooking
1 onion, diced
1 pork sausage, meat removed from the skin or 150 g (5½ oz) minced (ground) pork shoulder
150 g (5½ oz) minced (ground) beef
150 g (5½ oz) minced (ground) chicken or turkey
50 g (1¾ oz) fine fresh breadcrumbs
1 small bunch flat-leaf (Italian) parsley
10 sage leaves
1 free-range egg
1 cup (100 g/3½ oz) grated Grana Padano cheese
salt and freshly ground black pepper

Sauce
2 tablespoons olive oil
2 tablespoons unsalted butter
1 onion, diced
1 clove garlic, diced
200 g (7 oz) minced (ground) beef
200 g (7 oz) minced (ground) pork
1 rabbit liver or 150 g (5½ oz) chicken livers, chopped
6 anchovy fillets, roughly chopped
2 tablespoons capers, rinsed and drained
1 tablespoon freshly ground black pepper

Jim's Wet-roasted Rabbit with Herbs and Pecorino

Rabbit is a great ingredient to practise your butchery skills on.
Its make-up is similar to pork and lamb, and butchering a rabbit or a hare
allows you to develop a feel for the joints and muscles. Rabbit is also a
very versatile animal; every time I cook one, I do it differently. I add the cuts at
different times so everything cooks to perfection, but if you want to just
get it in the oven and relax, you can, and the dish will still be fine.

Preheat the oven to 160°C (315°F/Gas 2–3).

Follow the instructions for breaking down the rabbit, on page 135 up to step 7. Using a meat cleaver, chop the saddle across the bone into 3–4 pieces, depending on the size of the rabbit.

Heat a little olive oil in a large ovenproof saucepan over high heat. Add the rabbit legs and cook until golden. Remove from the pan. Add the saddle pieces to the pan and turn to seal on all sides until golden, then remove. Seal the rib pieces and remove.

Add the butter, carrot, garlic, onion, celery and thyme to the pan and cook until the butter starts to colour. When it is a dark brown, add the wine (carefully, as it may spit), then simmer until the liquid has reduced by half. Add the stock and return the rabbit legs to the pan, then bring to the boil and cover. Remove from the heat and transfer immediately to the oven to cook for 30 minutes.

Next, add the saddle pieces to the pan and cook for a further 30 minutes. Add the ribs and continue cooking for 5–10 minutes – you may need to top up with more stock if the sauce has reduced, the rabbit needs to be covered at all times. Remove the pan and make sure the leg meat is tender and coming off the bone.

Remove from the oven and sprinkle with the parsley, basil and pecorino while the rabbit is still hot. Serve in the pan with olive oil and crusty bread at the table.

Serves 2–4

1 x 1.2–1.5 kg–800 g (2 lb 10 oz–2 lb 5 oz) farmed rabbit

olive oil, for cooking

1 tablespoon unsalted butter

1 carrot, finely diced

6 cloves garlic, chopped

1 onion, chopped

3 sticks celery, finely chopped

5 sprigs thyme

1 cup (250 ml/9 fl oz) pinot grigio or other dry white wine

4 cups (1 litre/35 fl oz) Chicken Stock (page 191)

½ bunch flat-leaf (italian) parsley, chopped

10 basil leaves

1½ cups (150 g/5½ oz) grated pecorino cheese

crusty bread, to serve

extra-virgin olive oil, to serve

Breaking Down the Rabbit

Jim ～ I first learnt how to break down whole animals by practising on rabbit and hare – once you've mastered the technique, the basic mechanics are the same for lamb, pork and beef. This step-by-step guide will give you a good indication of the basic cuts or portions of most animals you are likely to cook. You will need a sharp boning knife, and a pair of kitchen scissors.

Step 1
Remove the front and back legs of the rabbit.

Step 2
At the first rib closest to the back legs, make an incision and cut all the way up through the belly, following the rib. Repeat on the other side.

Step 3
Snap the saddle off the rib cage and twist to remove. You may have to do a bit of cutting, but the saddle should come off easily. In some recipes you may leave this whole or may need to break it down into smaller portions for cooking – be guided by individual recipes and use your common sense.

Step 4
Using a meat cleaver, cut the tail piece off the saddle.

Step 5
Halve the rib cage by cutting along the spine using a pair of kitchen scissors.

Step 6
On the inside of the separated ribs, scrape your knife against the membrane holding the ribs to the belly, so that all the connective tissue is removed. Do this thoroughly on all the ribs.

Step 7
Using your right hand, hold on to the flap that is on the opposite side of the loin at the end of the ribs, and hold the loin end with your left hand (do the opposite if you are left-handed). Peel the belly backwards off the ribs and the ribs should pop out. Peel all the way down to the loin and remove the belly using your knife – you will be left with a perfect rabbit rack.

Step 8
On the saddle, make a long incision on either side of the spine and carefully cut along the bone to remove each loin.

Step 9
Remove the belly from the loins.

You should now have two back legs, two front legs, two loins, two racks, some belly trim and a tail piece.

There is very little wastage when breaking down a rabbit in this way. If you do have bits that are not required (the tail piece, for example), use them in a stock (wild rabbit especially makes exceptional stock). If your recipe doesn't use the belly, it is delicious pan-fried until cooked and then sliced and fried in oil as a crispy accompaniment to a dish. Some chefs even make layered terrines out of them. The belly can also be left on the loin and stuffed, rolled and then poached.

Jim~ My Perfect Roast Chicken (page 138) is a three-technique recipe in which we brine the chicken, poach it using a steeping technique after which it is chilled, and then roasted from cold so the chicken is crisp on the outside but beautifully moist on the inside. It requires quite a bit of preparation but the steps are very simple. If you don't have the luxury of an extra day to brine the chicken, leave it out. It is not entirely essential but is a great way of adding flavour to the meat. The chicken can be eaten after step two as a poached bird.

Chicken

Stefano ⌁ Jim's chicken is very cheffy. It is not for everyday, which is where I come in (page 139).

Jim's Perfect Roast Chicken

Serves 4–6

1.6 kg (3 lb 8 oz) whole free-range
    chicken, legs trussed
Brine (page 185)
1 stick lemongrass, bruised
1 handful thyme
2 sprigs rosemary
1 handful sage
2 lemons, cut in half
1 head garlic, cut in half
¼ cup (60 ml/2 fl oz) olive oil
freshly ground black pepper

Place the chicken in a large deep bowl with the brine for 3–4 hours.

Heat a large saucepan of lightly salted water over high heat with the lemongrass, thyme, rosemary and half the sage. Bring to the boil. You will need four times the amount of liquid to chicken, so the saucepan must be large enough to hold about 5 litres (175 fl oz) water and the chicken without overflowing.

Stuff the lemon halves and the garlic into the chicken cavity. Add to the boiling water and return to the boil. Remove from the heat and weigh the chicken down with a plate so it is fully submerged. Cover the saucepan with a lid and leave for 45 minutes.

Remove the chicken from the saucepan and discard the cooking liquid and flavourings. Transfer to an ice bath to chill. Once cool, refrigerate, uncovered, for a few hours or overnight to dry out the skin.

Preheat the oven to 220°C (425°F/Gas 7).

Place the chicken in a roasting tin and stuff the remaining sage into the cavity. Rub a little olive oil all over the chicken and season with pepper. (The brine should have sufficiently seasoned the chicken, so there is no need for additional salt.) Roast the chicken in the oven for 15–20 minutes until well coloured. Remove and let the chicken rest for about 10–15 minutes before carving and serving.

Simple Roast Chicken, the Stefano Way

Serves 4

1.6 kg (3 lb 8 oz) whole free-range
   chicken
100 g (3½ oz) salted butter, softened
12 sage leaves, chopped
1 tablespoon chopped rosemary
3 tablespoons chopped preserved
   lemon
olive oil, for cooking
salt
6 cloves garlic

Preheat the oven to 180°C (350°F/Gas 4).

With a sharp knife, separate the chicken skin from the breasts and the breast-bone (you will notice by inserting your fingers that the skin is still attached to the central bone either side of the breasts).

In a bowl, mix together the butter, sage, rosemary and preserved lemon. Use your fingers to push the butter under the skin and spread it around as evenly as possible – the butter should not be too soft and runny but still hold its shape when pressed onto the skin. Rub the chicken skin with olive oil and season lightly with salt.

Place the chicken on its side in a baking dish. Scatter around the garlic cloves and roast for 20 minutes, then turn the chicken on its other side and roast for another 20 minutes Finally, turn the chicken so it is sitting upright in the tray and cook for a further 20 minutes. Remove from the oven and rest for 10 minutes before carving.

Squeeze the garlic out of its skin and mix with the cooking juices, then pour over the chicken when carved. Apply extra salt if needed, but less is usually more.

Whole Fried Quail

This recipe is loosely based on a Chinese cooking technique that first poaches the bird gently and lets it dry slightly before frying. The aromatic stock will impart the flavour of the spices into the bird. This recipe is as unpretentious as it is fantastic. You take some jumbo quail and a few simple ingredients and you are in business. This recipe can be adapted to cook most poultry and game.

Serves 4

8 cups (2 litres/70 fl oz) Aromatic Stock
    (page 190)
4 whole quails, legs trussed
vegetable oil, for deep-frying
2 tablespoons sliced red chillies (if you like
    it hot, use bird's eye chillies)
4 cloves garlic, thinly sliced
1 bunch spring onions (scallions), sliced

Put the stock in a large saucepan or stockpot and bring to the boil. Add the quails and reduce the heat to low. Poach the quails for 15 minutes without boiling. Remove the quails and refrigerate, uncovered, overnight (or for a few days) for the skin to really dry out. You can cook them straight away and the results are great, but the skin will not be as crisp.

Preheat the oil to 180°C (350°F) in a deep-fryer or large heavy-based saucepan. Test the oil by dropping a small piece of bread in it – if it sizzles furiously it is hot enough.

Deep-fry the chilli and garlic until crisp, then remove with a slotted spoon and place in a bowl with the spring onion.

Deep-fry the quails, in batches, until very crisp. Remove and drain on paper towel.

To serve, cut each quail in half through the breastbone and serve with the fried chilli mixture.

Stefano ⁓ *This method is not Italian, but we are sure it would not be frowned upon by any of our Italian friends, especially those fond of garlic, chilli and quail.*

Trippa al Pomodoro

Tripe is available from most good butchers and can be ordered
ahead of time and kept frozen.

Serves 6

1 kg (2 lb 4 oz) tripe, cut into 1 cm (½ inch)
    strips
olive oil, for cooking
2 brown onions, chopped
½ head garlic cloves
2 sticks celery, chopped
1 carrot, chopped
1 cup (250 ml/9 fl oz) white wine
1⅔ cups (400 g/14 oz) tinned Italian
    tomatoes
1 tablespoon tomato paste (concentrated
    purée)
1 piece butt-end of prosciutto or pancetta,
    or a chunky bit of either
8 cups (2 litres/70 fl oz) Chicken Stock
    (page 191)
grated Parmigiano Reggiano, to serve
chopped flat-leaf (Italian) parsley, to serve

Bring a saucepan of lightly salted water to the boil and blanch the
tripe for 10 minutes – this is done to purify them a little more.
Drain well.

Meanwhile, heat a little olive oil in a saucepan over medium heat.
Add the onion, garlic, celery and carrot and cook until the onion
has softened. Add the tripe and wine, then add the tomatoes, tomato
paste, prosciutto and some stock. Simmer very gently for several
hours with the lid askew. Add just enough stock to keep moist but
never drown the tripe, and keep adding as this evaporates fairly
quickly. Tripe may take up to 5 hours to soften.

Remove from the heat, divide between serving plates and sprinkle
the Parmigiano Reggiano and parsley on top to serve.

*Stefano ⁓ For a whole generation of Australians who had tripe in white sauce
imposed on them by their parents, this classic Italian tripe dish is the one that
reconciles them with this special offal. It also pleases those who have been afraid
to try eating tripe and converts them, due, in large part, to an appreciation of
this much-undervalued ingredient. I know this from experimenting with diners
over the years. When I offer* trippa al pomodoro *as a complimentary extra,
about 70 per cent of people are enlivened by the dare, some are not moved by it,
but only a few dislike it outright.*

Four Dishes, One Duck

Jim ~ The following recipes came about because I don't like waste, and it is a great feeling when you can make something to eat using every part of an animal – here I use the breast, neck, bones and legs of the duck. Rendered duck fat is available for purchase at most good butcher shops. There will always be leftover fat from roasting; it can be reused, so keep it in an airtight container in the refrigerator and use in place of oil or butter.

Serves about 5

Breaking down the duck

Step 1
Buy whole ducks with the neck and skin intact. Cut around the neck just above the wishbone. Don't cut through the neck bone, just the skin. Hold the whole duck with one hand and pull the neck skin off. With your other hand push it inside out and remove and discard any veins or glands and rinse the neck skin under cold water. This will be the skin for the sausage.

Step 2
Remove one side of the meat from the carcass by making an incision down one side of the breast-bone. Keeping your knife close to the carcass, cut through the wing joint and pop the thigh bone out by pushing it up with your fingers. Cut through the thigh joint and remove the leg, breast and wing in one piece. Repeat on the other side.

Step 3
Separate the wings from the breasts, then separate the leg and the breast by cutting the skin that connects them. Score the breast lightly; I do it diagonally across the breast but please yourself.

Duck Broth

2 duck carcasses
1 bunch thyme
1 bay leaf
1 small knob ginger
1 carrot, split lengthways
1 stick celery, roughly chopped
1 onion, quartered
200 ml (7 fl oz) port
1 head garlic, cut in half
1 star anise
8 cups (2 litres/70 fl oz) Chicken Stock (page 191)

Preheat the oven to 200°C (400°F/Gas 6).

Place the duck carcasses on a roasting tin (chopped if you wish) and roast until golden brown, about 20 minutes. Add all the other ingredients, making sure there is enough stock to over the duck carcasses – top up with a little water if needed. Cover the tin tightly with 3 layers of foil – this will help to minimise evaporation. Reduce the oven temperature to 140°C (275°F/Gas 1) and cook for 5 hours. Remove from the oven and strain the broth, discarding the bones and vegetables. When ready to serve, skim off any excess fat, reheat the broth and bring to the boil to heat through.

Duck Legs

2 duck legs
salt and freshly ground black pepper
4 sprigs thyme
3 cloves garlic
500 g (1 lb 2 oz) duck fat

Preheat the oven to 120°C (235°F/Gas ½).

Place the duck legs in an ovenproof roasting tin and season with salt and pepper. Add the thyme and garlic and cover with the duck fat. Cover the tray with foil and cook for 4 hours, or until the flesh is tender and pulls away from the bone. Remove from the oven and let the duck cool in the fat. It can be refrigerated almost indefinitely stored in the fat.

Increase oven temperature to 190°C (375°F/Gas 5).

Remove the legs from the fat and remove the small thigh bone. Clean up the top of the leg bone using a knife and roast for 5–8 minutes or until hot and the skin is crisp. Alternatively, the legs can be browned in a hot pan just before serving.

Pan-fried Duck Breasts

2 scored duck breasts (see step 3, previous page)
salt and freshly ground black pepper

Preheat the oven to 180°C (350°F/Gas 4). Place a frying pan over low heat. Season the duck breasts and add to the pan, skin side down. Place a light weight, such as a plate or pan on top of the breast to help keep the skin flat and also to help the fat render. Continue cooking for 10 minutes on low heat, pouring the fat away as it accumulates in the pan. Transfer the pan to the oven without turning and roast for 8 minutes. Remove from the oven, turn the breast over and rest for 15 minutes before slicing. Serve with roasted potatoes and a nice salad, garnished with figs or cherries. A multitude of garnishes love duck.

Easy Duck-neck Sausage

½ chicken breast, diced
1 clove garlic, crushed
1 tablespoon diced pancetta
50 ml (1¾ fl oz) pouring (whipping) cream
1 free-range egg white
4 sage leaves, chopped
salt and freshly ground black pepper
the skin of 1 duck neck (see step 1, previous page)

Preheat the oven to 200°C (400°F/Gas 6). Bring a large saucepan of water to the boil. When the water boils, reduce the heat so the water isn't boiling but remains hot.

Place all the ingredients, except the duck neck skin, into a food processor, season with salt and pepper, and process to a coarse paste. You can cook a little of the filling, if you like, and taste for seasoning.

Spoon the filling into a large piping bag and pipe into the neck skin.

Wrap the sausage in plastic wrap, roll into a tight cylinder and tie both ends to maintain a nice shape. Poach in the hot water for 20–30 minutes. Remove the sausage then refrigerate. When the sausage is cold and set, place on a baking tray and bake until the skin is nice and brown, about 15 minutes. Slice and serve.

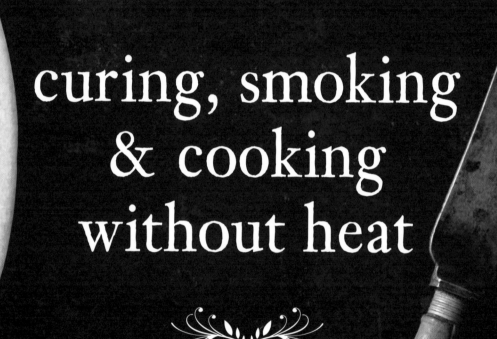

curing, smoking
& cooking
without heat

Jim~

Curing, salting and smoking were traditionally born out of the need to preserve foods before refrigeration, for travelling or for storing foods through seasons that were less than abundant.

These techniques now make up some of the most important aspects of many cuisines. It is impossible to comment on or even realise the infinite ingredients that have been spawned by this style of cookery. In the modern world of food, these are invaluable techniques for gaining textures and flavours from certain ingredients. It is very satisfying to produce a lovely piece of cured meat from scratch.

Stefano~

I have never familiarised myself with the art of smoking food, but I have certainly enjoyed the results of this process. For example, a 'ham' made out of older lamb made by traditional Aussie butchers, and slightly smoked, is something to behold.

The late Gianni Gianfreda from Jonathan's in Melbourne was a true innovator. He used to thunder on about the use of cheap and nasty smoking chips used by large food manufacturers, and this served to diminish my interest and made me wary. Jim has made me re-evaluate this time-honoured technique and he has shown me some fantastic possibilities with smoked butter, beef and salmon.

I am now reading how in some parts of Italy they used to mince lamb, season it like salami, work it into small bread-loaf shapes, coat it with a thick polenta crust, and smoke it inside their huge fireplaces. There is a project in sight.

Jim's Flat Pancetta

I love pancetta for many reasons, although I only recently attempted to
make my own. I was prepared for the project to go wrong, but to my surprise
the end result was extremely good. It is now all we use in the restaurant.
This recipe is foolproof: just make sure the pork is sufficiently cured before drying,
and don't dry it in a place that is too hot – it needs to dry slowly.

Makes 2.5 kg (5 lb 8 oz)

4 cloves garlic, peeled

14 g (½ oz) sodium nitrate

50 g (1 oz) salt

30 g (1 oz) raw (demerara) sugar

2 teaspoons (10 g/⅜ oz) fennel seeds

4 bay leaves

½ teaspoon grated nutmeg

3 sprigs thyme

2 tablespoons (40 g/1½ oz) black
    peppercorns

1 large pork belly (about 2.5 kg/5 lb 8 oz),
    ribs removed

Use a spice grinder or mortar and pestle to grind the garlic, sodium
nitrate, salt, sugar, fennel seeds, bay leaves, nutmeg, thyme and half
of the pepper to make a powder.

Line a tray with plastic wrap with enough overhang on each side to
enable you to wrap the pork. Evenly spread half of the cure mixture
over the bottom of the tray.

Place the pork on the cure mixture, skin side down, and cover with
remaining the cure. Fold the plastic wrap over the pork to loosely
wrap it, trying to make sure the cure is touching the flesh. Leave
for at least 1 week in the refrigerator for the pork to become firm.
Unwrap the pork and rinse thoroughly.

Coat the flesh with remaining ground pepper. At each end of the
belly, use a sharp knife to pierce a small hole in the flesh and use
some kitchen string to thread through so that you can securely hang
the pork.

Hang the pancetta in a cool, humid place (not the refrigerator) for a
further 1 week until the meat is dry and very firm. Store unwrapped
in the refrigerator for up to a month and slice as needed.

Stefano ⁓ *I am declaring a ban on imitation pancetta – that meat roll with
no fat that is typically sold in most supermarkets. Pancetta without fat has no
purpose in the kitchen, especially when it is used to wrap anything to be roasted.
It is worthwhile learning how to make pancetta or where to buy the real thing.
It makes the best tomato-based sauces for pasta and is wonderful in* spaghetti
alla carbonara.

Lardo

Lardo is pork belly fat cured with salt. Melted over bread or polenta it is exceptionally moreish. These days, good-quality lardo is served sliced, much the same as prosciutto, to have with warm bread. In small quantities, it is delicious. Lardo is great for melting in a non-stick pan and frying with a couple of eggs.

Place the pork back fat on a clean work surface and season with pepper.

Place half of the salt on a large baking tray. Arrange the bay leaves over the salt and place the pork fat on top. Cover with the remaining salt and refrigerate for about 2 weeks.

Remove and pat the cure off with a tea towel.

The lardo can then be hung to dry at room temperature for up to 2 months as is the tradition, but I tend to use it as is.

The lardo keeps well if kept covered in the refrigerator. I usually serve it draped over a scallop or an egg or use it as an aromatic base for a stock or sauce. Chopped up finely with rosemary and sage, lardo can also be used to braise ducks or chickens, as a sofrito. It is also useful to 'lard' meats – as the word suggests – particularly game or to line the sides of a terrine.

Makes 2 kg (4 lb 8 oz)

2 kg (4 lb 8 oz) piece pork back fat
2 tablespoons (20 g/¾ oz) freshly ground
    black pepper
4 kg (9 lb) coarse salt
10 bay leaves

Guanciale (Cured Pork Cheek)

Guanciale has a fat content between lardo and pancetta. It is far easier and less time consuming to make than pancetta. Guanciale is so versatile: it works well with scallops and fruits like peach, fig and melon. It is also great to use as part of a base with aromatic vegetables in a sauce or soup. It is essential for pasta *matriciana*.

Place all the ingredients except the pork cheeks in a large bowl and mix well to combine. Put a layer of the cure mixture on the bottom of a deep baking tray and arrange the pork on top, skin side down. Cover with the remaining cure. Cover with plastic wrap and refrigerate for 4–5 days – the cure will go to liquid after one day; this is fine as the cheek still cures.

When cured, rinse the pork under cold water and pat dry.

At the end of each cheek, use a sharp knife to pierce a small hole in the flesh and use some kitchen string to thread through so that you can securely hang the pork.

Hang the guanciale for 7–10 days in a cool, humid place until very firm to the touch. Remove the dry and tough outer skin and slice by hand or use a meat slicer – enjoy with pickles and bread.

Makes 1 kg (2 lb 4 oz)

300 g (10½ oz) table salt
300 g (10½ oz) caster (superfine) sugar
5 cloves garlic, smashed
30 g (1 oz) black pepper, lightly crushed
½ bunch thyme, stems and all, chopped
½ teaspoon sodium nitrate
2 large pork cheeks, about 500 g (1 lb 2 oz) each

Stefano ‿ *Imagine this: I am conducting a cooking demonstration in the Hobart Auditorium with the Tasmanian Symphony Orchestra. They have just finished performing the theme from* The Godfather *with a piano accordion and all.*

I then present the conductor with ... a pig's head (a horse's head not being available).

I then explain that the pig's cheeks, cured with salt, become guanciale and proceed to demonstrate a spaghetti matriciana. After much banter, the auditorium returns to silence. I slice the guanciale and put the pan on the flame. Then I throw in the sliced guanciale – peppery, salty, fragrant. As the slices hit the pan (with a little oil), an explosion of fragrance literally travels through the auditorium, just like sound!

I will never forget the 1200 audience members responding with a uniform sigh of collective pleasure. It was a spectacular and memorable experience.

Classic Cold Smoked Salmon

Store-brought smoked salmon is a hit-and-miss affair; it is sometimes hard to tell a good product from a bad one, because it is impossible to know the quality of the fish that was used for smoking or the quality of the other ingredients. When making your own, you have control over all these elements, and the result is always excellent. You can use ocean trout or other fish, but you need to make sure you alter the curing time to the size of the fillet. It is hard to specify an exact time frame, because the thickness of the fish dictates the time it takes. The rule of thumb is that, when it is ready, the fish should be quite firm in the fattest part.

Makes 1.5 kg (3 lb 5 oz)

1 kg (2 lb 4 oz) Basic Cure (page 184)
1.5 kg (3 lb 5 oz) piece of salmon, pin-boned, skin on
2 tablespoons ground fennel seeds
½ bunch dill, chopped
200 g (7 oz) wood smoking chips

Place half the Basic Cure in a baking tray of similar size to the fish. Place the fish, skin side down, on the cure.

Season the flesh on top with the fennel and dill and cover with the remaining cure mixture – the fish must be buried for effective results. Wrap with plastic wrap and place in the refrigerator for 24 hours.

Remove the salmon after 24 hours and rinse well to remove the cure mixture.

Put the smoking chips in a deep roasting tin and place over high heat until the chips are smoking furiously. You can use a stovetop but this may smoke out your house, so an outdoor barbecue is the best option. Meanwhile, place the salmon in a perforated baking tray that will fit inside the roasting tin with the chips. When the chips are smoking, remove from the heat and place the tray with the salmon in it on top. Cover with more foil if there is smoke escaping. Leave for 20–30 minutes for the smoke to infuse. If you prefer a strong smoke flavour, turn the salmon over and repeat this smoking step.

Wrap the fish in clean plastic wrap and refrigerate until ready to use. The fish keeps well for 2–3 weeks, but it rarely lasts that long because works well for breakfast, lunch and dinner!

Salt Cod

This recipe was devised as an alternative to real salt cod; we use it in *baccalà mantecato* or creamed cod. Using this recipe in place of traditional cod gives a fresher flavour and it can be prepared faster, without the need to wash the cod for two to three days before using.

Makes 500 g (1 lb 2 oz)

500 g (1 lb 2 oz) salt
200 g (7 oz) caster (superfine) sugar
3 sprigs of thyme
zest of 1 lemon
1 teaspoon fennel seeds
500 g (1 lb 2 oz) white cod fillet (blue-eye is good but any other cod works well)

Mix all of the ingredients together, except the cod, in a non-reactive baking tray that will be a snug fit for the cod. Bury the cod fillet in the cure mixture and refrigerate for 18–20 hours.

Remove the cod and rinse well in cold water.

The fresh nature of this product means it cannot be stored for very long, as it still contains moisture which can harbour bacteria – it is best eaten within a few days of being made.

Homemade Duck Ham

This is a fresh ham, not air-dried, so there is no need for the use of sodium nitrate. This means the ham spoils faster, so eat it within a week or so of curing. The ham is not smoked, but you can do so if you wish, just use the cold-smoking technique used for the smoked salmon on page 154.

In a large bowl, mix together the Basic Cure and all of the remaining ingredients, except the duck breasts. Place half of the cure mixture in the base of a non-reactive baking tray. Arrange the duck breasts on top and cover with the remaining cure mixture. Refrigerate for 18–20 hours, or until the duck is quite dry, with just a little give when you press on it. Remove and use paper towel to pat off the cure – I don't wash it because the cure adds to the taste.

To serve, thinly slice the duck by hand or use a meat slicer, slicing across the grain. Serve as part of an antipasto platter or as a starter with bread, crackers and pickles.

Makes about 500 g (1 lb 2 oz)

500 g (1 lb 2 oz) Basic Cure (page 187)
½ bunch thyme
5 juniper berries, crushed
2 bay leaves
10 whole black peppercorns, crushed
2 duck breasts

desserts

Stefano~

There is a varied selection of traditional Italian dessert in this chapter as well as something new. The influence of different cuisines and methods intersect and merge, reflecting the many cultures that have occupied the Italian peninsula over the centuries, from the endemic poverty of rural areas (which even managed to turn pig's blood into a delicious soft pudding), to the influence of adjoining countries – France, Austria, Switzerland, Greece and other Mediterranean

Jim~

A dessert can make or break a dining experience. As the last course served, it is often the most memorable.

Modern pastry is a very exciting area for a chef to be involved in these days. New equipment and products such as liquid nitrogen, hot gelling agents, minus grills, cream guns, blast chillers, Pacojets and Thermomixes, just to name a few, are now common components in any restaurant pastry section. Innovative machinery and products do not make us better cooks, but they do enable us to push the boundaries of creativity. It is only our imagination that limits us.

This section consists mostly of simple recipes, and thankfully you will not be called upon to handle liquid nitrogen. These desserts are designed to be achieved without too much hassle, and they also offer some good foundations while introducing some interesting ideas.

Yoghurt Mousse

This lovely mousse is obviously white, so you could line a mould with slices of strawberries for colour or, if you don't like the fuss, simply place the whole mousse in a bowl to serve, and spoon it out with berries on the side. This dessert works a treat with honey-flavoured beers. Try it, you will see how well a dessert can work in conjunction with beer rather than a dessert wine.

Put the milk and sugar into a saucepan over medium heat and heat to 90°C (190°F/Gas ½), or just under boiling point – check using a kitchen thermometer. Remove from the heat. Squeeze any excess water from the gelatine and whisk into the hot milk until dissolved.

Beat the cream to semi-soft peaks, then slowly add the honey, beating only until just combined.

Pour the milk mixture into the yoghurt, then fold the yoghurt into the honey and cream to combine.

Spoon the mousse mixture into eight 100 ml (3½ fl oz) capacity dariole moulds, tapping to remove any air bubbles and smooth the surface. Refrigerate for several hours.

To serve, invert the mousses onto serving plates and garnish with fruit, either fresh or puréed.

Makes at least 8

100 ml (3½ fl oz) full-cream (whole) milk
¼ cup (50 g/1¾ oz) caster (superfine) sugar
4 sheets gold-strength gelatine sheets,
    soaked in cold water for 20 minutes
300 ml (10½ fl oz) pouring (whipping) cream
50 g (1¾ oz) honey, preferably orange
    blossom
1 cup (250 g/9 oz) plain yoghurt
fruit, such as strawberries, raspberries or
    kiwi fruit, to serve

Blood Orange and Macadamia Cake with Honey Curd

This cake is simple and fast to make, and to top it off it is gluten and dairy free. This cake is moist and delicious. The honey curd is rich, so if you are health conscious, leave it out and serve the cake with a little orange compote or syrup.

Serves 8

3 blood oranges
3 × 55 g (2 oz) free-range eggs
200 g (7 oz) caster (superfine) sugar
1⅓ cups (200 g/7 oz) toasted macadamia
    nuts, roughly chopped
3 cups (300 g/10½ oz) ground almonds
1 teaspoon baking powder
zest of 1 blood orange
pouring (whipping) cream, to serve (optional)

Honey Curd
100 g (3½ oz) honey
4 × 55 g (2 oz) free-range eggs
115 g (4 oz) unsalted butter, cubed

To make the Honey Curd, put the honey and eggs in a small saucepan over low heat. Gently heat the eggs, whisking constantly until the mixture has thickened, about 15 minutes. Remove from the heat and add the butter, a cube at a time, whisking to combine after each addition. Place in a container or jug and refrigerate until cool.

Preheat the oven to 170°C (325°F/Gas 3). Grease and flour eight 150 ml (5 fl oz) capacity ramekins.

Place the whole oranges in a saucepan and pour in enough water to cover. Weight them down with a plate to ensure they remain submerged. Place the pan over high heat and bring to the boil for about 10 minutes. Drain the water, pour in enough fresh water to cover and bring back to the boil for a further 10 minutes. Repeat this step two or three more times to ensure most of the bitterness is cooked out of the oranges. Remove from the heat, allow to cool slightly, then transfer to a food processor and process until smooth.

Using an electric mixer fitted with a paddle attachment, beat the eggs and the sugar until thick and pale.

Combine the macadamia nuts, ground almonds and baking powder in a large bowl and add the egg mixture, stirring to combine. Add the puréed oranges and the orange zest and use a rubber spatula to fold all of the ingredients together until well combined. Pour into the prepared ramekins and bake for 15–20 minutes, or until a skewer inserted comes out clean. Remove from the oven and turn out onto a wire rack to cool.

Serve with the honey curd and some cream, if desired.

Jim's Chocolate and Olive Oil Tart

The teaming of chocolate and olive oil is not a new concept at all: the grassy olive oil and chocolate are perfect together. The olive oil acts to enrich the chocolate and makes it super silky and is also a lot better for you than butter. It's a win–win situation, so why not?

To make the Sweet Pastry, place the sugar and butter in an electric mixer fitted with a paddle attachment. Beat until pale and thick. Add the egg, beating well. Sift together the baking powder and flour into a bowl. Add the butter mixture and use your hands to bring the pastry together. Knead for about 5 minutes, or until a smooth pastry dough forms. Wrap in plastic wrap and refrigerate for at least 1 hour.

Preheat the oven to 180°C (350°F/Gas 4). Grease a 30 cm (12 inch) loose-bottomed flan (tart) tin with baking paper.

Roll the pastry out between two sheets of baking paper until it is about 5 mm (1/4 inch) thick. Discard the baking paper and line the flan tin with the pastry. Trim the overhanging edges. Line the pastry shell with baking paper, fill with rice or baking weights, and blind bake the pastry for 10–15 minutes. Remove and discard the paper and weights and bake for a further 4–5 minutes, until golden. Remove from the oven and set aside to cool slightly.

To make the Chocolate Filling, bring a large saucepan of water to the boil. Put the milk, cream and chocolate in a heatproof bowl and set over the pan making sure the base of the bowl does not touch the water. When the chocolate has melted, add the eggs and, using a whisk, stir continuously until the mixture is quite hot, about 70°C (150°F) is ideal – check using a kitchen thermometer. Remove from the heat and whisk in the olive oil – it should emulsify.

Pour in the chocolate mixture into the pastry in the tin while it is still warm. If you allow it to cool down too much it will set and you will not get a lovely even top and a nice shine. If the chocolate mixture has set, just place it back over the boiling pot of water until it is runny again.

Allow the tart to set in the refrigerator for at least 3 hours or overnight before slicing and serving.

Serves 8–10

Sweet Pastry

⅓ cup (80 g /2¾ oz) caster (superfine) sugar
100 g (3½ oz) unsalted butter, softened
1 × 55 g (2 oz) free-range egg
½ teaspoon baking powder
1⅔ cups (250 g/9 oz) plain (all-purpose) flour

Chocolate Filling

150 ml (5 fl oz) full-cream (whole) milk
100 ml (3½ fl oz) pouring (whipping) cream
250 g (9 oz) dark chocolate (at least 40% cocoa), chopped
2 × 55 g (2 oz) free-range eggs
150 ml (5 fl oz) extra-virgin olive oil

Tiramisu

Jim ~ Meringues are not a traditional component of tiramisu but I have added them to my recipe (page 170) for a nice crunch and for aesthetic reasons. The plating of this dessert can be left to you. Many of the components can be made ahead and stored.

Stefano ～ My tiramisu (page 171) uses chocolate stout instead of coffee. Stout is not new in dessert. However, my chocolate stout, Choc Hops, made by the Mildura Brewery, is – even if I say so myself – very good.

Jim's Deconstructed Tiramisu

Serves 4–6

1 cup (250 ml/9 fl oz) fresh
   espresso coffee

Meringue Cylinders
1 quantity Swiss Meringue
   (page 179)
2 tablespoons unsweetened cocoa
   powder

Coffee Crumbs
1 quantity Chocolate Frangipane
   (page 196)
1 teaspoon ground coffee

Mascarpone Cream
200 g (7 oz) mascarpone
150 ml (5 fl oz) pouring (whipping)
   cream
1 tablespoon caster (superfine) sugar

Marsala Anglaise
½ cup (125 ml/4 fl oz) Marsala
1 quantity Basic Anglaise (page 196)

Preheat the oven to 120°C (235°F/Gas ½). Line a tray with baking paper. To make the Meringue Cylinders, place the meringue in a piping bag fitted with a 1.5 cm (⅝ inch) nozzle. Pipe cylinders along the length of the tray. Cut the cylinders into 3 cm (1¼ inch) lengths. This will not be a completely clean cut but it will be enough to snap the meringues when they are done. Place into the oven and cook for 3 hours. Remove and separate each of the cylinders. Allow to cool. Put the cocoa into a sieve and dust the meringues liberally. Set aside.

Preheat the oven to 130°C (250°F/Gas 1). Line a tray with baking paper. To make the Coffee Crumbs, break the Frangipane into pieces and place on the tray. Bake in the oven until dry and crisp (this could take a few hours). Set aside two-thirds of the frangipane pieces to use for the tiramisu. Place the remaining frangipane in a food processor with the coffee and process to a powder. Set aside.

To make the Mascarpone Cream, whisk together the mascarpone, cream and sugar until it stiffens. Refrigerate until needed.

To make the Marsala Anglaise, add the Marsala to the Basic Anglaise while it is still hot. Chill until needed.

To assemble, soak the frangipane pieces in the coffee for a few seconds – you don't want the cake to be too soggy. Place a mound of the coffee crumbs on serving plates and add a few chunks of the soaked cake and a few quenelles of the mascarpone cream. Garnish with some of the meringue cylinders. Flood the plate with marsala anlgaise and serve.

Stefano's Chocolate Stout Tiramisu

Serves 6

3 free-range egg yolks

300 g (10½ oz) mascarpone

100 ml (3½ fl oz) pouring (whipping) cream

50 g (1¾ oz) icing (confectioner's) sugar

6 ladyfinger (savoiardi) biscuits, cut in half lengthwise, then in half again

1 cup (250 ml/9 fl oz) chocolate stout

Dutch cocoa powder, for dusting

Place the egg yolks, mascarpone, cream and sugar, all as cold as possible, in the chilled bowl of an electric mixer fitted with a whisk attachment and beat at medium speed until well combined and creamy. Keep chilled if not using immediately.

Spoon half the mixture into a large serving bowl, or use a piping bag to pipe the mixture into the bottom of six ramekins or individual serving dishes. Place half of the biscuits over the cream base and brush gently with chocolate stout. Keep brushing until the biscuits are well soaked. Repeat the layering process.

Before serving, sprinkle with the cocoa powder. This tiramisu is ideal served with chocolate beer.

Quick Mascarpone Mousse with Rhubarb

This is designed as a very quick light dessert to serve after a big meal. The mousse is extremely simple and goes well with any kind of fruit. The rhubarb can be stored in its syrup for up to a week. If you prepare the fruit ahead of time, this dessert can be on the table in less than ten minutes.

Serves 6

100 g (3½ oz) caster (superfine) sugar
1½ tablespoons (30 ml/1 fl oz) grenadine
1 vanilla bean, split lengthways and seeds
    scraped
3 sticks rhubarb, cut into 2.5 cm (1 inch)
    lengths

Mascarpone Mousse
300 ml (10½ fl oz) pouring (whipping) cream
⅔ cup (150 g/5½ oz) caster (superfine)
    sugar
300 g (10½ oz) mascarpone
juice of 1 orange
finely grated zest of 1 orange
2 tablespoons honey

Combine the sugar, grenadine and vanilla bean and seeds with 100 ml (3½ fl oz) water in a small saucepan over medium heat and stir to dissolve the sugar. Add the rhubarb and poach gently for 15 minutes, or until the rhubarb is soft.

To make the Mascarpone Mousse, combine all of the ingredients in a mixing bowl and pour into a cream whipper and charge twice. Alternatively, beat with an electric mixer until firm peaks form. Refrigerate until needed.

To serve, divide half the rhubarb between six serving glasses. Top with the mousse and then the remaining rhubarb.

Simple Panna Cotta

Jim ⁓ This is my version of the infamous panna cotta. In my mind, panna cotta is like a catchy song that gets over-played on the radio and starts to lose its appeal; yet at the same time, it gets stuck in your head for days. It is an accomplishment to make something memorable out of something so simple – after all, it is essentially set cream. I infuse the cream with a few coffee beans, and some orange and vanilla to give it some subtle complexity.

Place the cream, milk, sugar, orange juice, orange zest, Grand Marnier, coffee beans and vanilla bean and seeds into a saucepan. Set over low heat until hot but not boiling and stir until the sugar has dissolved. Remove from the stove. Squeeze any excess water from the gelatine and whisk into the hot cream until dissolved. Set aside for at least 10 minutes for the flavours to infuse.

Pour the cream mixture into a bowl set over a bowl of ice and allow to cool, whisking every few minutes. After about 15 minutes the cream will be ready to be poured into moulds. Strain the mixture through a fine sieve and pour into a jug.

Lightly grease ten 100 ml (3½ fl oz) capacity dariole moulds. Fill the moulds two-thirds of the way with the cream and refrigerate for about 3 hours to set.

To serve, invert the moulds into serving plates and serve with fresh or poached fruit, if desired.

Serves 10

600 ml (21 fl oz) pouring (whipping) cream
150 ml (5 fl oz) full-cream (whole) milk
150 g (5½ oz) caster (superfine) sugar
juice of ½ orange
finely grated zest of ½ orange
30 ml (1 fl oz) Grand Marnier or Cointreau
2 coffee beans
1 vanilla bean, split lengthwise and seeds
    scraped
3 titanium-strength gelatine leaves, soaked
    in cold water for 20 minutes
fresh or poached fruit, to serve (optional)

Saffron Panna Cotta

This panna cotta is the perfect example of how savoury ingredients
can be used in desserts. This can be served as a pre-dessert in a little egg cup
(the saffron pana cotta representing the yolk and the yoghurt the white)
or as a main dessert served in coffee cups or ramekins.

Serves 4 (or 15 as a pre-dessert)

15 egg shells, trimmed carefully and washed
thoroughly (optional)

Yoghurt Foam
700 g (1 lb 9 oz) plain yoghurt
300 ml (10½ fl oz) pouring (whipping) cream
150 g (5½ oz) caster (superfine) sugar

Coffee Crumbs
100 g (3½ oz) Chocolate Frangipane
(page 196)
1 teaspoon ground coffee

Panna Cotta
300 ml (10½ fl oz) pouring (whipping) cream
⅓ cup (80 ml/2½ fl oz) full-cream (whole)
milk
⅓ cup (80 g /2¾ oz) caster (superfine)
sugar
2 coffee beans
1 vanilla bean, split lengthwise and seeds
scraped
1 teaspoon saffron threads
2 sheets gold-strength gelatine leaves,
soaked in cold water for 20 minutes

To make the Yoghurt Foam, combine all of the ingredients in a
cream whipper and charge twice, or beat with an electric mixer until
soft peaks form. Refrigerate until needed.

To make the Coffee Crumbs, place the cooked Chocolate Frangipane
in a food processor and process to make a fine powder. Mix with the
coffee and set aside.

To make the Panna Cotta, place the cream, milk, sugar, coffee
beans, vanilla bean and seeds and saffron into a large saucepan
over medium heat. When the cream almost comes to the boil,
remove from the stove. Squeeze any excess water from the gelatine
and whisk into the hot cream until dissolved. Set aside for at least
10 minutes for the flavours to infuse.

Pour the cream mixture into a bowl set over a bowl of ice and allow
to cool, whisking every few minutes. After about 15 minutes the
cream will be ready to be poured into moulds. Strain the mixture
through a fine-mesh sieve. Return the saffron to the panna cotta
and whisk to combine.

If serving in egg shells, place the shells in an egg carton and fill two-
thirds of the way up with the saffron mixture. Alternatively, divide
the mixture between four ramekins or serving glasses. Refrigerate
for 3 hours to set.

Top each panna cotta with yoghurt foam and sprinkle generously
with the coffee crumbs.

Bonet: A Piedmontese Crème Caramel with Savoiardi and Amaretti

Piedmont is the region of origin of the famous – or infamous – panna cotta.
It is also the region of this home-style dessert, which is easy to make and satisfying to eat.
Bonet is a crème caramel, which sets easily on account of the solids it contains.
A perfect dessert for the home.

Serves 12

4 cups (1 litre/35 fl oz) full-cream (whole)
   milk
100 g (3½ oz) ladyfinger (savoiardi) biscuits,
   crushed
120 g (4¼ oz) amaretti biscuits, crushed
50 ml (1¾ fl oz) espresso coffee
2 tablespoons Marsala or port
2 tablespoons rum
5 × 55 g (2 oz) free-range eggs
370 g (13 oz) caster (superfine) sugar
2 tablespoons unsweetened Dutch cocoa
   powder, sifted
caster (superfine) sugar, extra

Preheat the oven to 160°C (315°F/Gas 2–3).

Put the milk in a saucepan and bring to the boil until it has reduced by one-quarter, about 3 cups (750 ml/25 fl oz). Remove from the heat and allow to cool.

Add the biscuits, coffee, Marsala and rum to the milk.

In a large bowl, beat together the eggs and 2/3 cup (150 g/5½ oz) of the sugar until pale, then add the sifted cocoa. Pour the milk mixture into the bowl with the eggs and sugar and gently combine.

Put the remaining sugar into a saucepan with a little water and cook over high heat until a nice dark caramel forms. Pour into the base of twelve 150 ml (5 fl oz) capacity ramekins. Place the ramekins in a roasting tin and set aside to cool.

Pour the milk mixture into the ramekins in the tin. Pour in enough water to come three-quarters of the way up the side of the ramekins. Cook in the oven for 40–45 minutes, or until set. Remove from the oven and allow to cool, then refrigerate for 2 hours, or until ready to serve.

Milena's Crostata

An easy pastry dessert for those afternoons when you want something sweet with your tea or coffee. Crostata is delicious fresh out of the oven with a generous dollop of double cream.

Preheat the oven to 180°C (350°F/Gas 4). Line the base of a 23 cm (9 inch) flan (tart) tin with baking paper.

Put the flour in the bowl of an electric mixer fitted with a whisk attachment. Add 2 of the eggs, one at a time, beating well after each addition. Add the sugar, salt, liqueur, butter and just enough milk to make a soft pastry.

Roll the pastry out between two sheets of baking paper so it is about 5 mm (¼ inch) thick. Use the pastry to line the base and side of the prepared tin, trimming the edges to fit.

Fill the pastry case with jam. Roll out the remaining pastry and cut out strips. Place diagonally over the tart in one direction, then another to form a lattice pattern on top. Lightly beat the remaining egg and brush the pastry top.

Bake the crostata for 35–40 minutes, until golden. Remove from the oven, allow to cool in the tin for 10 minutes before turning out onto a wire rack to cool completely.

Serves 8–10

2 cups (300 g/10½ oz) plain (all-purpose) flour
3 × 55 g (2 oz) free-range eggs
150 g (5½ oz) caster (superfine) sugar
a pinch of salt
50 ml (1¾ fl oz) liqueur, such as brandy or grappa
80 g (2¾ oz) unsalted butter, softened
80–100 ml (2½–3½ fl oz) full-cream (whole) milk
300 g (10½ oz) jam

Passionfruit Curd Tart with Burnt Meringue

These are funky little tarts obviously influenced by their more popular cousin, the lemon meringue. Any citrus or acidic fruits are good for this recipe, and when it comes to piping the meringue it is really up to you – as long as it is even and you can get a nice dark crust (like a toasted marshmallow). Weigh the eggs for this tart: accuracy is crucial to its success.

Preheat the oven to 170°C (340°F/Gas 3).

Roll out the pastry to make a large square, about 5 mm (¼ inch) thick. Cut into quarters and use each quarter to line the base and side of four 10 cm (4 inch) round flan (tart) tins. Line the pastry shells with baking paper, fill with rice or baking weights, and blind bake the pastry for 10–15 minutes, until golden. Remove and discard the paper and weights and bake for a further 4–5 minutes. Do not cook until it is too dark – you want it to be crisp but not hard. Remove from the oven and set aside to cool.

To make the Passionfruit Curd, combine the eggs, sugar and passionfruit pulp in a saucepan over low heat. Cook for about 15 minutes, stirring continuously, until the mixture coats the back of a wooden spoon and is nice and thick. Remove from the heat and add the butter, piece by piece, stirring to incorporate after each addition. Squeeze any excess moisture out of the gelatine and add the gelatine to the mixture. Whisk to combine then set aside to cool slightly.

Pour the passionfruit curd evenly between the prepared tart shells and refrigerate for at least 2 hours, or until set.

To make the Swiss Meringue, bring a small saucepan of water to the boil. Place the sugar and eggs into a heatproof bowl, stir with a whisk to combine, then set over the pan and heat the mixture for about 30 minutes or until it reaches about 80°C (160°F) – check with a kitchen thermometer. Remove from the heat and whisk until the mixture is cool and stiff. Spoon the meringue into a piping bag fitted with a fine nozzle and pipe over the top of each passionfruit tart in small teardrop shapes until the whole surface is covered.

Use a kitchen blowtorch to colour the meringue. If you don't have a blowtorch, preheat a griller (broiler) to high and place the tarts under for a few minutes until lightly browned.

Makes 4

1 quantity Sweet Pastry (page 167)

Passionfruit Curd
2 sheets titanium-strength leaf gelatine, soaked in cold water for 20 minutes
100 g (3½ oz) free-range eggs
100 g (3½ oz) caster (superfine) sugar
100 g (3½ oz) passionfruit pulp
30 g (1 oz) unsalted butter, cubed

Swiss Meringue
200 g (7 oz) caster (superfine) sugar
100 g (3½ oz) free-range egg whites

Frittole di Carnevale

Stefano ⁓ This is an infallible recipe used by Anna, my mother-in-law. These fritters, or *frittole*, are eaten in Italy at carnival time, which is a period when people are allowed to play and indulge, right up until Ash Wednesday, which marks the beginning of Lent. In Australia, we are not bound so much by tradition, so you can eat these anytime, preferably hot and dusted with coarse sugar.

Makes 20

2 cups (300 g/10½ oz) self-raising flour
1 cup (170 g/6 oz) sultanas (golden raisins)
a pinch of salt
¼ cup (55 g/2 oz) sugar, plus extra
    for dusting
a few drops of natural vanilla extract
2 tablespoons Grand Marnier liqueur
equal quantities olive oil and vegetable oil,
    for deep-frying

Place all of the ingredients, except the oil, in a large bowl and stir together with just enough water to make a soft batter. Set aside for 2 hours.

Preheat the oil to 180°C (350°F) in a deep-fryer or large heavy-based saucepan. Test the oil by dropping a little batter in it – if it sizzles furiously it is hot enough. Drop in tablespoons of batter at a time, in batches, and deep-fry until golden brown.

Remove the fritters from the oil using a slotted spoon and drain on paper towel. While they are still hot, roll them in the sugar to coat. Serve hot.

Apple Tea Cake

Stefano ⁓ This is one we have used in the de Pieri family since forever. This is a modified recipe to suit Australian ingredients. This may seem unbelievable, but Italian flour and yeast translated into Australian equivalent quantities just made a mess of this cake. I turned it, as usual, to my mother-in-law, who played around with it until we got this recipe right. But, for me it's not quite the same, which goes to show that it is not easy to recreate a flavour memory and general impressions from one place to another. So, if anything, it goes to show that we are always forced to modify and adapt our experiences.

Preheat the oven to 190°C (375°F/Gas 5). Lightly grease a 23 cm (9 inch) ring cake tin with butter and dust with a little flour.

In a bowl, cream together the butter and sugar for a few minutes until pale and creamy. Beat in the eggs, then add the grappa and finally the sifted flour. Pour the mixture into the cake tin, making sure it is evenly distributed.

Peel the apples, remove the cores and slice thinly. If you do this ahead of time, sprinkle a little sugar on the apples to prevent them from discolouring. Arrange the sliced apples over the top of the cake batter in the tin, pushing them into the batter a little.

Bake in the oven for about 45 minutes, or until a skewer inserted into the centre of the cake comes out clean. Remove from the oven and allow to cool in the tin for 10 minutes, before turning out onto a wire rack to cool completely. Cut into slices and serve.

Serves about 15

150 g (5½ oz) unsalted butter, softened, plus extra for greasing

200 g (7 oz) caster (superfine) sugar, plus extra for sprinkling

3 free-range eggs

50 ml (1¾ fl oz) grappa or brandy

1⅓ cups (200 g/7 oz) self-raising flour, sifted

2 Granny Smith apples

basics

Seasoning

The art of seasoning is not simply adding salt or pepper. To my mind, seasoning encompasses a broad range of ingredients that all work together to bring balance to a dish. These include salt, acid, texture, spice, cream and other additions.

Throughout this book you will read instructions to season with lemon juice and olive oil or with parmesan and salt flakes. Parmigiano Reggiano is quite expensive, so use it only if you wish to. Parmigiano, or its less expensive cousin, Grana Padano, is a more generic cheese, and usually not aged a great deal. It still does the job very well. It is up to you to choose.

All ingredients add different flavours and textures; whether it be a different grain of salt or a stronger olive oil, they all contribute differently to the seasoning of a dish. It is only through tasting that the cook can really understand the importance and reasoning behind the art of balance and seasoning. So no measurements are given when referring to salt and pepper or in some cases lemon juice or oil and the like. Your senses are there for a reason – use them and decide yourself.

Blanching

The basic salt-to-water ratio for cooking vegetables and pasta is about 1 tablespoon salt for every 4 cups (1 litre/35 fl oz) water. We tend to use a bit more salt but this is the rule of thumb in the restaurant world; the home cook probably prefers less. Salt helps retain chlorophyll in green vegetables and also seasons the ingredient. It is impossible to get the same effect from seasoning a dish after it has been prepared.

Basic Cure

This is a dry cure, in which you bury the meat. It works exceptionally well with fish – cure for about 24 hours for large fish – but is also great for most red meats.

Makes 1 kg (2 lb 4 oz)

700 g (1 lb 9 oz) salt
300 g (10½ oz caster (superfine) sugar

Mix the sugar and salt together in a large bowl. Add herbs, citrus zest or any other aromatics as you wish.

Brining

Brining uses the principal of osmosis, which roughly means the natural flow of liquids into each other. In a natural and passive environment, salt flavours the meat and the meat naturally flavours the water in a kind of organic equalisation.

Brining helps to denature proteins and unravel them, adding to tenderness. The addition of salt and sugar also enables the meat fibres to hold on to moisture as well as seasoning the meat.

This is a general brine that can be used for poultry and other meats. Aromatic ingredients can be added to the brine to enhance flavours.

Makes 4 litres

245 g (8½ oz) salt
130 g (4½ oz) sugar

Combine the salt and sugar in a large saucepan or similar container with 4 litres (140 fl oz) water. Submerge the meat in the liquid, allowing for 2–3 hours for every 1 kg (2 lb 4 oz). Remove the meat, rinse well, pat dry with paper towel and cook as you like – it is that easy!

Parmesan Crisps

Makes 4

1½ cups (150 g/5½ oz) grated Parmigiano Reggiano

Preheat the oven to 190°C (375°F/Gas 5) and line a tray with baking paper. Place four mounds of grated parmesan on the paper and spread them out to about the size of the bottom of a drink can. Bake for about 10 minutes until the cheese has melted and is starting to crisp. Remove from the oven and allow to cool until you can peel them from the paper. As they cool they will crisp up.

Clarified Butter

This is difficult to do with less than 500 g (1 lb 2 oz) of butter, but it keeps for a very long time refrigerated.

Makes 500 g (1 lb 2 oz)

500 g (1 lb 2 oz) butter

Bring a saucepan of water to the boil. Place the cold butter in a small stainless steel bowl that fits over the pan without touching the water. Reduce the heat to low and leave until the butter has melted and the milky solids come to the top. Skim using a small ladle. Repeat until the solids are all discarded.

Truffle Butter

Makes about 150 g (5½ oz)

150 g (5½ oz) unsalted cultured butter
5 g (⅛ oz) black truffle, diced (truffle paste will work fine
    for this)
a pinch of sea salt

Take the butter out of the fridge and allow to come to room temperature. Add the truffle and season with salt. Store rolled in plastic wrap or wrapped in baking paper in the refrigerator.

Smoked Butter

Makes 500 g (1 lb 2 oz)

good handful of wood smoking chips
500 g (1 lb 2 oz) unsalted cultured butter, frozen

Put the smoking chips in a small pot or pan. Place the butter in a perforated tray that will fit inside the pan with the chips. Cover with foil, plastic wrap or another tray and place over high heat until the chips are smoking furiously (you don't want them to be on fire because you will melt the butter). You can use a stovetop but this may smoke out your house, so an outdoor barbecue is the best option. Turn off the heat and leave for 20–30 minutes for the smoke to infuse. Remove the butter and freeze again before repeating this smoking step two or three times until the butter smells and tastes smoky. Refrigerate to set before using; dice into 2 cm (¾ inch) cubes.

Boiled Eggs

1½ tablespoons salt
100 ml (3½ fl oz) vinegar
5 free-range eggs

Put the salt and vinegar into a saucepan with 8 cups (2 litres/70 fl oz) water and bring to the boil. Add the eggs and cook for 5 minutes for soft-boiled eggs or 11 minutes for hard-boiled. Remove, cool and peel.

Boiled Quail Eggs

1½ tablespoons salt
100 ml (3½ fl oz) vinegar
12 quail eggs

Put the salt and vinegar into a saucepan with 8 cups (2 litres/70 fl oz) water and bring to the boil. Add the eggs and cook for 2 minutes and 20 seconds for soft-boiled eggs and 3 minutes 20 seconds for hard-boiled. Remove, cool and peel.

Béchamel Sauce

This makes a nice velvety sauce. If you want it thicker, increase the quantity of flour and butter by half.

Makes 4 cups (1 litre/35 fl oz)

4 cups (1 litre/35 fl oz) full-cream (whole) milk
80 g (2¾ oz) plain (all-purpose) flour
100 g (3½ oz) unsalted butter
½ teaspoon freshly grated nutmeg
salt and freshly ground black pepper

Put the milk into a saucepan and bring to the boil.

In a separate saucepan, combine the flour and butter and place over medium heat. When the butter has melted, add the milk, one ladle at a time, stirring until smooth after each addition. Initially the flour, butter and milk will turn into a ball. Keep adding milk until the ball slowly turns to a glossy paste and eventually a creamy sauce. Use a wooden spoon so you can reach all parts of the bottom of the pan, where the milk and flour can catch and burn. If your béchamel burns it will be ruined, so watch the pot like a hawk and stir constantly.

Continue until all of the milk is added. Reduce the heat and cook, stirring occasionally, for about 30 minutes or until the raw taste of flour has gone. Add the nutmeg, and salt and pepper. Allow to cool.

Mayonnaise

The thing to remember about mayonnaise is that it is an emulsion and refers to the incorporation of a fat into a liquid. Eggs have a strong emulsifying quality because the yolk contains a large amount of lecithin. The acid from the vinegar helps to stabilise the emulsion and add flavour. If the mayonnaise does split, start again from scratch and when underway, slowly add the split sauce so it is not wasted.

Makes 2 cups (500 g/1 lb 2 oz)

4 free-range egg yolks
1 tablespoon white wine vinegar or lemon juice
1 tablespoon Dijon mustard (optional)
2 cups (500 ml/17 fl oz) vegetable or grapeseed oil
salt and freshly ground black pepper

Place the yolks, vinegar and mustard, if using, into a large bowl or the bowl of an electric mixer fitted with a whisk attachment. Slowly drizzle in the oil in a steady stream, whisking constantly to combine. (If using an electric mixer, set the speed to medium.) If the mayonnaise becomes too thick as you incorporate the oil, just add a little warm water. When all the oil is incorporated, taste for seasoning, adjusting with salt, pepper and some more vinegar if needed.

VARIATION: To make horseradish mayonnaise, combine 100 g (3½ oz) of the mayonnaise with ⅔ cup (60 g/2¼ oz) freshly grated horseradish in a bowl, adding a little extra, to taste, if desired.

Pickled Onion Mayonnaise

Makes 2 cups (500 g/1 lb 2 oz)

2 large onions, finely sliced
80 g (2¾ oz) salt
200 ml (7 fl oz) white vinegar
⅓ cup (80 g/2¾ oz) caster (superfine) sugar
2 cups (500 g/1 lb 2 oz) Mayonnaise (left)

Place the onion in a bowl and add the salt. Mix to coat evenly, cover with plastic wrap, and leave to marinate for at least 1 hour in the refrigerator. After 1 hour, the onion should be wilted. Wash under cold water to remove the salt.

Place the vinegar and sugar in a saucepan over low heat, stirring until the sugar has dissolved. Pour the hot syrup over the onion and allow to cool. The onion can be stored indefinitely, so a large batch can be made and stored in containers or jars.

Strain the pickling liquid from the onion and reserve for the mayonnaise.

Make the Mayonnaise following the instructions in the recipe on the left, replacing the vinegar with 3 tablespoons of the pickling liquid. When all the oil is incorporated, add the onion and mix together to combine. Taste for seasoning, adjusting with salt pepper and some extra pickling liquid, if needed.

Yabby Oil

Makes 2 cups (500 ml/17 fl oz)

2 cups (500 ml/17 fl oz) vegetable or olive oil (or use a
    combination of both)
1 carrot, chopped
1 small onion, chopped
1 stick celery, chopped
2 tablespoons tomato paste (concentrated purée)
12 raw yabby (freshwater crayfish) shells
2 star anise
a pinch of saffron (optional)

Heat a little vegetable oil in a small saucepan and
add the carrot, onion, celery and tomato paste.
Cook for 10 minutes, or until quite dark. Add
the yabby shells and all of the remaining oil to
submerge the shells. Add the star anise and saffron,
reduce the heat to low, and cook slowly for about
3–4 hours, to extract the maximum amount of
colour from the shells.

Place a strainer over a large container and use a tea
towel or oil filter to line the strainer. Strain the oil,
discarding the shells and flavourings. The oil can
be stored in an airtight glass jar in the refrigerator
indefinitely. If you can't keep it refrigerated, use
within 2 weeks.

Fish and Olive Oil Velouté

*The first thing to remember with this recipe is
that it is an emulsion and relies on the body in
the stock to be stable. I have added a small amount
of soy lecithin, which helps the emulsification
and will help stabilise the velouté. It can be
purchased in most health food shops. This
velouté is to be used straightaway and must stay
warm after the oil is incorporated. Prepare the
base stock and only add the oil just before serving.*

Makes 800 ml (28 fl oz)

2 cups (500 ml/17 fl oz) Fish Stock (page 193)
2 cups (500 ml/17 fl oz) Chicken Stock (page 191)
2 sprigs thyme
1 teaspoon soy lecithin
1 cup (250 ml/9 fl oz) olive oil
juice of ½ lemon
salt

Place the Fish and Chicken stocks and the thyme in
a saucepan over high heat and cook until the liquid
has reduced to about 300 ml (10½ fl oz). Remove
from the heat and strain. While the stock is still hot,
stir in the lecithin.

Using a hand-held stick blender, slowly add the
oil in a thin, steady stream with the blender on
medium speed, as if making a mayonnaise. Strain,
if necessary, then season to taste with lemon juice
and salt.

Court Bouillon

Makes 12 cups (3 litres/105 fl oz)

3 cups (750 ml/25 fl oz) dry white wine
2 bay leaves
1 onion, peeled and chopped
½ bunch thyme
1 small carrot, peeled and chopped
80 g (2¾ oz) salt
1 small lemon, sliced
1 small orange, sliced
1 stick celery, chopped

Place all the ingredients in a saucepan with 12 cups (3 litres/105 fl oz) water and bring to the boil.

Remove, allow to cool and place in the refrigerator until needed. Do not strain – I like to leave all the aromatics in when poaching.

Alternatively, you can use the stock immediately. This stock can be re-used 3–4 times for poaching but it must be strained after each use. Store in an airtight container in the refrigerator for up to 2 weeks or in the freezer for up to 6 months.

Aromatic Stock

Makes about 8 cups (2 litres/70 fl oz)

5 cups (1.25 litres/44 fl oz) Chicken Stock (see opposite)
100 g (3½ oz) grated palm sugar (jaggery)
150 ml (5 fl oz) port or Madeira
3 pieces dried orange or mandarin peel
1 tablespoon dried chilli flakes
5 pieces liquorice root
3 star anise
1 cinnamon quill
2 whole cloves
1 head garlic, cut in half crosswise
1 large knob ginger, sliced

Place all of the ingredients in a large saucepan and bring to the boil for 15 minutes.

Remove, allow to cool and place in the refrigerator until needed. Do not strain – I like to leave all the aromatics in when poaching.

Alternatively, you can use the stock immediately. This stock can be re-used 3–4 times for poaching but it must be strained after each use. Store in an airtight container in the refrigerator for up to 2 weeks or in the freezer for up to 6 months.

Vegetable Stock

Makes 8 cups (2 litres/70 fl oz)

3 sticks celery, chopped

2 carrots, peeled and chopped

1 onion, peeled and chopped

2 sprigs tarragon (optional)

1 sprig basil (optional)

3 sprigs thyme (optional)

1 star anise (optional)

3 whole black peppercorns

1 cup (250 ml/9 fl oz) dry white wine

1 good-quality vegetable stock cube (bouillon), crushed

Place all of the ingredients in a large saucepan with enough water to cover. Place over low heat and bring to a simmer, then cook for 30 minutes. Remove from the heat and strain before using. Store in an airtight container in the refrigerator for up to 2 weeks or in the freezer for up to 6 months.

Chicken Stock

Chicken stock means different things to different people. In this book, unless specified, it means chicken bones (or chicken boilers), slowly boiled in water with carrots, celery, onions and salt. The purpose of cooking slowly is to allow the fat and any impurities to come to the top without boiling back into the stock. This is then skimmed off during cooking.

Some salt must be introduced from the start for the flavour to develop properly. You can always add more if needed. On the other hand, if you add only at the end, as is often taught at various cooking schools, it will not taste right.

The stock must be clear, flavoursome and golden. Only then can you use it for things like risotto and soups. Cooked with small Italian pasta, it makes a great minestra – *a dish virtually unknown outside Italian homes, but one of the ultimate comfort foods.*

Makes 8 cups (2 litres/70 fl oz)

5 chicken frames

1 carrot, chopped

1 celery stick, chopped

1 onion, peeled

5 whole black peppercorns

1 tablespoon coarse salt

Place all ingredients in a large saucepan with 4 litres (140 fl oz) water and slowly bring to the boil, skimming off the fat and any scum that rises to the surface during cooking. Simmer for at least 2 hours, then remove from the heat, strain and use as directed. Store in an airtight container in the refrigerator for up to 2 weeks or in the freezer for up to 6 months.

Beef Stock

Makes 8 cups (2 litres/70 fl oz)

2 large beef leg bones or joint knuckles (get your butcher to
    saw them into manageable 5 cm/2 inch pieces)
150 ml (5 fl oz) vegetable oil
2 carrots, peeled and halved
2 onions, peeled and chopped
3 sticks celery, chopped
3 tablespoons tomato paste (concentrated purée)
3 cups (750 ml/25 fl oz) red wine
2 sprigs rosemary
1 head garlic, cut in half crosswise
2 bay leaves

Preheat the oven to 200°C (400°F/Gas 6). Place
the bones in a roasting tray and roast until well
coloured, about 20–30 minutes.

Heat the vegetable oil over high heat in a large
saucepan or stockpot big enough to hold all the
bones. Add the carrot, onion and celery and cook
for 10 minutes, or until they are nicely browned.

Add the tomato paste and continue to cook – there
needs to be quite a bit of oil or the tomato will
burn. Cook until the tomato paste is a really dark
red. Add the wine and reduce by half, then add the
bones and herbs and pour in enough water to cover.
Bring to the boil, then reduce the heat to low and
cook for at least 8 hours (although if you have the
time and patience it is best cooked for 24 hours),
skimming off the fat and any impurities that rise to
the surface.

Remove from the heat and strain before using.
Store in an airtight container in the refrigerator for
up to 2 weeks or in the freezer for up to 6 months.

Dark Lamb Stock

Makes 8 cups (2 litres/70 fl oz)

3 kg (6 lb 12 oz) lamb bones (get your butcher to saw them into
    manageable 5 cm/2 inch pieces)
150 ml (5 fl oz) vegetable oil
2 onions, peeled and chopped
2 carrots, peeled and halved
3 tablespoons tomato paste (concentrated purée)
3 sticks celery, chopped
3 cups (750 ml/25 fl oz) red wine
2 sprigs rosemary
1 head garlic, cut in half crosswise
2 bay leaves

Preheat the oven to 200°C (400°F/Gas 6). Place
the bones in a roasting tray and roast until well
coloured, about 20–30 minutes.

Heat the vegetable oil over high heat in a large
saucepan or stockpot big enough to hold all the
bones. Add the carrot, onion and celery and cook
for 10 minutes, or until they are nicely browned.

Add the tomato paste and continue to cook – there
needs to be quite a bit of oil or the tomato will
burn. Cook until the tomato paste is a really dark
red. Add the wine and reduce by half, then add the
bones and herbs and pour in enough water to cover.
Bring to the boil, then reduce the heat to low and
cook for at least 8 hours (although if you have the
time and patience it is best cooked for 24 hours),
skimming off the fat and any impurities that rise to
the surface.

Remove from the heat and strain before using.
Store in an airtight container in the refrigerator for
up to 2 weeks or in the freezer for up to 6 months.

Fish Stock

Makes 8 cups (2 litres/70 fl oz)

1 large fish skeleton from a firm white-fleshed fish, such as cod or snapper (do not use the bones from an oily fish, such as tuna, because they are too strongly flavoured)
1 fennel bulb, chopped
1 onion, peeled and chopped
1 star anise
1 teaspoon fennel seeds
1 cup (250 ml/9 fl oz) dry white wine
1 lemon, halved
3 stems flat-leaf (Italian) parsley
a splash of Pernod

Remove the eyes from the fish head. Cut out the gills using a pair of scissors. Wash the skeleton under cold water until the water runs clear. Chop the bones into 5 cm (2 inch) pieces and place in a large saucepan or stockpot with the fennel, onion, star anise, fennel seeds and wine. Pour in enough water to cover and place over medium heat. Bring to the boil, then reduce the heat to low and simmer for 30 minutes, skimming off any impurities that rise to the surface.

Remove from the heat and add the lemon, parsley and a splash of Pernod. Cover the pan with a lid and allow to stand at room temperature for 15 minutes. Strain the stock and use as directed.

Store in an airtight container in the refrigerator for up to 4 days or in the freezer for up to 6 months.

Crayfish and Kombu Broth

Makes 5 litres (175 fl oz)

7 crayfish spiders or leftover crayfish carcasses
1 cup (250 ml/9 fl oz) vegetable oil
1 carrot, peeled and chopped
2 large fennel, chopped
2 onions, peeled and chopped
3 sticks celery, chopped
2/3 cup (150 g/5½ oz) tomato paste (concentrated purée)
350 ml (12 fl oz) Pernod or pastis
350 ml (12 fl oz) brandy or cognac
8 cups (2 litres/70 fl oz) Chicken Stock (page 191)
8 cups (2 litres/70 fl oz) Fish Stock (left)
2 pinches saffron threads
2 star anise
3 large sheets dried kombu
oyster sauce (optional)

Preheat the oven to 190°C (375°F/Gas 5). Place the crayfish carcasses on a baking tray and roast for 25 minutes. Remove and chop or smash up the shells a little.

Heat the vegetable oil in a large saucepan or stockpot over medium–high heat. Add all of the vegetables and cook until coloured. Add the tomato paste and continue to cook until a very dark red, stirring continuously. Add the carcasses and mix, then add the Pernod and brandy, and flame the alcohol using a lighter. When the flames die down, add the Chicken and Fish stocks, the spices and kombu and bring to the boil, then reduce the heat to low and simmer for 2–3 hours.

Remove from the heat and strain, then pass again through a fine seive lined with a tea towel or oil filter. Season with some oyster sauce, if desired, which will add to the *umami* flavour.

Napoli Sauce

Makes 4 cups (1 litre/35 fl oz)

olive oil, for cooking
1 small onion, peeled and diced
4 cloves garlic, smashed
3¼ cups (800 g/1 lb 12 oz) tinned whole tomatoes
5 large basil leaves
100 ml (3½ fl oz) olive oil
salt and freshly ground black pepper
sugar (optional)

Heat a little olive oil in a saucepan over medium heat. Add the onion and garlic and cook until translucent and tender, about 5 minutes.

Strain the tomatoes over a bowl, reserving the liquid. Squeeze the tomatoes to remove the seeds and add the pulp and all of the liquid to the pan, along with the basil. Cook for 30–40 minutes over low heat, or until the tomatoes break down.

Remove from the heat and use a hand-held stick blender to blend until smooth. Add the oil, salt and pepper. It may need a pinch of sugar if the tomatoes are quite tart.

Simple Pizza Dough

Makes 1 kg (2 lb 4 oz), or enough for 4 pizzas

2 cups (500 ml/17 fl oz) full-cream (whole) milk
2 teaspoons sugar
2 teaspoons (7 g/¼ oz) active dried yeast
4 cups (600 g/1 lb 5 oz) plain (all-purpose) flour
1 teaspoon salt
50 ml (1¾ fl oz) olive oil

Place the milk and sugar in a saucepan over low heat and heat it to about 60°C (140°F) – it should never be hot enough to boil, but the idea is to get it to a temperature that is sufficient to kickstart the yeast – use a kitchen thermometer to check. Add the yeast to the warm milk and whisk to combine.

Put the flour, salt and olive oil in a mixing bowl. Make a well in the centre and pour in the milk mixture. Gently mix with a fork. As it starts to come together, knead with your hands and keep kneading until a smooth, elastic dough forms. Cover with a clean, damp tea towel and leave in a warm place for 30 minutes or until doubled in size.

To make pizzas, separate the dough into 4 pieces and roll out into circles on a lightly floured work surface. Transfer to a lightly oiled tray, top with your favourite toppings and bake in a preheated 220°C (425°F/Gas 7) oven for 10–15 minutes until the pizza base is cooked.

Polenta

Makes 500 g (1 lb 2 oz)

50 g (1¾ oz) salt
3⅓ cups (500 g/1 lb 2 oz) yellow polenta
2 cups (200 g/7 oz) grated Parmigiano Reggiano (optional)

Line a 40 cm × 20 cm (16 inch × 8 inch) baking tray with plastic wrap. Put the salt and 8 cups (2 litres/70 fl oz) water in a saucepan and bring to the boil. Add the polenta, very slowly, whisking constantly. Reduce the heat to low and cook for around 30 minutes, or until the polenta is no longer grainy, whisking occasionally. When the polenta is cooked, whisk in the cheese, if using, and mix thoroughly. Check the seasoning and add more salt if necessary.

Pour the polenta into the lined tray. You can either bake the polenta in a preheated 180°C (350°F/Gas 4) oven and serve warm, or refrigerate until set (about 2 hours) and cut the polenta into slices to serve cold, or pan fry in a little olive oil until crisp.

Homemade Pasta

Makes 8 serves

3⅓ cups (500 g/1 lb 2 oz) '00' flour
6 × 55 g (2 oz) free-range eggs, lightly beaten

Put the flour in a bowl and make a well in the centre. Slowly add the eggs into the well, stirring constantly with a fork. When combined, turn the mixture out onto a clean work surface and knead until it forms a smooth silky dough. Cover with a damp cloth and rest for 1 hour.

Roll out the dough using a pasta machine to the desired thickness and cut into your desired style. (If you are making a filled pasta, such as ravioli or tortellini, add a little extra liquid before rolling – this can be achieved by adding another egg or a little water.)

Basic Anglaise

Makes 300 ml (10½ fl oz)

140 ml (4½ fl oz) full-cream (whole) milk
140 ml (4½ fl oz) pouring (whipping) cream
1 vanilla bean, split lengthwise and seeds scraped
3 free-range egg yolks
⅓ cup (80 g/2¾ oz) caster (superfine) sugar

Place the milk, cream, and vanilla bean and seeds in a saucepan over high heat.

Meanwhile, place the egg yolks and sugar in a bowl and whisk until combined and pale. When the milk mixture reaches boiling point, pour it over the eggs, whisking constantly. Return the mixture to a clean pan and reduce the heat to low. Stir with a wooden spoon until the mixture thickens slightly and is cooked – it needs to reach 80°C (160°F) – check using a kitchen thermometer, if you don't have a thermometer you can tell it is cooked when it coats the back of a wooden spoon and there is no detectable taste of raw egg.

Frangipane

Makes 750 g (1 lb 10 oz)

1 cup (250 g/9 oz) unsalted butter, softened
250 g (9 oz) caster (superfine) sugar
4 × 55 g (2 oz) free-range eggs, beaten
2½ cups (250 g/9 oz) ground almonds
½ cup (75 g/2¾ oz) plain (all-purpose) flour
100 g (3½ oz) unsweeteened cocoa powder (if making the chocolate version)

Preheat the oven to 170°C (325°F/Gas 3) and grease a slice tin.

In a large bowl, beat together the butter and sugar until pale and fluffy. Add the eggs, one at a time, beating well after each addition. Fold in the ground almonds and flour. If you are making a chocolate frangipane, add the cocoa and stir to combine.

Bake for 15–20 minutes, until a skewer inserted comes out clean. The frangipane can be eaten as is, or crumbled and dried to make a crumble. Frangipane can also be used as a filling for tarts and other pastries.

Index